PRODUCE
YOUR
LIFE

HOW TO HAVE A
CREATIVE CAREER
AND
FINANCIAL FREEDOM

Produce Your Life

How to Have a Creative Career AND Financial Freedom

Jeannie O'Neill

v.10.22.25

ISBN: 979-8-9997054-7-1 (paperback)

ISBN: 979-8-9997054-8-8 (hardcover)

Visit Jeannie at: Jeannie-ONeill.com

Contents

Tell me, what is it you plan to do
  with your one wild and precious life?

— Mary Oliver

Introduction

Everyone wants a creative career.

Well, maybe not *everyone*. But YOU do. That's why you picked up this book.

Most people let fear stop them. And their number one fear is not having this thing called "*security.*"

"Sure, I'd love to be a writer/actor/musician (fill in the blank with your own dream) but you can't *make a living* at it."

Sound familiar?

This is the book to show you how to be an artist, *without* starving. It's a survival guide for any creative person entering the workforce for the first time, or re-entering in a new capacity. It's about finding and doing the work you'll love, without sacrificing a decent quality of life. It's about encouraging you to have the life of your dreams.

The term "artist" as it's used here means *any kind of creative*—a producer, director, designer, content creator, dancer, writer, composer . . . anyone who makes their living in the creative space.

And we artists *need* a book like this. No one told your brother, who wanted to go into accounting, "Oh my God, *really?* Do you think you can make a *living* at it? Aren't you *scared?*"

People (even well-meaning friends and family) will tell you that choosing a creative, fun career is impractical. (John Legend's father wanted him to be a dentist. *A dentist!*) You may be wondering if they are right. Are you making a totally irresponsible choice that's going to leave you broke and unhappy? I don't think so. I believe that if being a creative is what's in your heart, it's the most reasonable, practical choice you can make. You're going to spend most of your life working, so you may as well enjoy it.

You can absolutely design a creative career and life you love. It happened for me. And it happened without personal connections or any big, lucky break. How? I made it happen. And I did it by adapting some of the methods I was learning in television production *to produce my life.*

For over thirty years I've made my living as a television producer, director, and writer. I can honestly say that I've never had a boring job, or one that wasn't creative. And I've never had a "day job" either.

I don't fit the profile of a "starving artist," and neither should you. I'm not willing to suffer for my craft. As an artist, you may not always make a lot of money. But you can absolutely have a creative career AND a high quality of life. You just have to make a few smart choices.

I have friends and colleagues making their living as actors, screenwriters, fashion designers, musicians—you name it. And we've all managed to do it without starving. You'll hear our stories in these pages. In fact, some of us travel the world for fun. Some of us live in homes we own (in California, no less!) while supporting spouses and kids. Some are killing it as digital nomads and influencers. You'll read profiles of artists as diverse as a professional opera singer in Michigan and a tattoo artist in Cholula, Mexico. Our stories will prove to you that achieving even a modest and unsteady income and having financial security are not mutually exclusive.

None of us got here by accident, however. We very deliberately set about making our dreams come true.

When I was starting out on my career path as a producer and director, I wanted a system to help me get where I wanted to be, in my career and in life. I wanted a formula for success. So I created one, using techniques I was learning about what it takes to get a TV show on the air.

Every production starts with a Big Idea. What is the show about? What's the story? Why go to all the effort of producing it? The Big Idea for you is the life you want. What's your story? In my case, I wanted to travel the world, have a vibrant social life, and love both my work and my free time. What do you want? Part One of this book, "What's The Big Idea?" will help you figure it out, then help you get your production up and running.

If you want to produce something big, be it a TV show, or a LIFE, it helps to stay on schedule and on budget.

In Part Two, "Let's Get This Show On The Road!" we'll delve into the mindset of a successful creative and what it takes to survive and thrive through the ups and downs of your chosen path—the layoffs and downsizing, the temptations of the highs, the various slings and arrows that come with a creative field and shifting economy.

Show me a producer who isn't good at handling money and I'll show you one who doesn't work very often. Money MATTERS—so, like any good producer, you've got to master this component as well, if you want to enjoy a high quality of life. Part Three: "Show Me The Money!" will cover how to acquire and manage the funds you need to make your vision reality.

People will tell you all sorts of things about how having a creative career with a non-traditional path and an atypical schedule aren't healthy or positive things. Don't you believe them. There's a lot of crap out there disguising itself as conventional wisdom, such as "Looking for a job is a full-time job." Poppycock. Been there, done that, and there's a better way, trust me. Together we'll explode these myths so that you can take advantage of this weird, wonderful, free-lance lifestyle and make it work for you.

If you know you want a creative career, if your heart beats just a little faster when you think about it, then this is the book for you. You *can* create the life of your dreams.

Part One

What's The Big Idea?

Chapter One

How to Figure Out What to Do with Your Life: Follow the Energy

"Follow your passion." "Find your bliss." Nice bumper stickers, but how do you *do* that? Thinking about this can be a lot. Especially in school, when they put all this pressure on you to KNOW and DECIDE and even DECLARE it. To THEM. They give you The Myers-Briggs personality test and send you to career fairs and all that. Ugh.

There's a much better way to find the career that will bring you the greatest joy and personal satisfaction.

And finding your right work is essential. Because you are going to spend most of the waking hours of your life working. It's imperative that you love it. I'm not saying you are going to love every minute of every job you'll ever have. You won't. But if you find your right work, you're way ahead of the game as far as being a happy, fulfilled, and successful person. And isn't quality of life what it's all about?

It's no accident that so many poets have written about this very subject. As contemporary American poet Mary

Oliver writes: *What are you going to do with your one, precious life?*

Or as thirteenth-century Islamic scholar and poet Rumi wrote: *Everyone has been made for some particular work and the desire for that work has been put in every heart.*

But how to do that?? If the world is your oyster, how to find your pearl? I think particularly for people who are very talented, there *are* many things you COULD do. How to decide? The good news is: There are clues everywhere.

If you were drawn to this book, odds are you are a particularly creative person. Therefore, I think YOU are uniquely qualified to make decisions intuitively. Sure, you can be all Aristotelian about it, or channel Ben Franklin and make a list of pros and cons, measuring this career against that one. Your analytic right-brain side will want to do just that, and be attracted to the logic in that process. BUT. There's a better way. One that will never let you down. And that is: *Follow the energy.* Okay, maybe you resist this idea because it sounds a little too woo-woo. Fair enough. But stay with me here.

Follow the energy. What does this *mean?* Simple. It means acting on what makes your heart beat a little faster. What are you drawn to? Perhaps you've heard the expression "The heart wants what it wants." Typically this expression is employed in the context of romance, but it applies to other things too. And you can trust this feeling. The dreams you dream, the longings, passions, fantasies that consume you, were placed in YOU for a reason: YOU. You see the world in a precise way that no one else does. Don't you think there's energy in that? And maybe wisdom? Divine wisdom, perhaps? There is. And that's why you can trust it.

Have you heard the expression "What's IN you is FOR you"? Don't discount your heart's desires as vain or silly or unimportant, or anything else dismissive. For therein lie the seeds of greatness.

My hiking buddy, Kristina, is a professional photographer. She grew up in Russia, and some of her earliest and fondest childhood memories are of her grandfather taking her to a portrait studio to get her photo taken every year as a young child. Something about that experience spoke to her. But she was also the only child of a single mom who struggled financially when they immigrated to Chicago. When she got to college, even though she wanted to be a photographer, her mom convinced her that it might be prudent to study something where she could "make some real money." So she got a business degree, went to New York, and got a job in marketing.

And then ... she took a photography class. And she LOVED it. She was hooked. The camera felt right in her hands. She spent ten hours at a time in the darkroom, and time flew by unnoticed. She left marketing to launch her own photography business and made her living doing that for the next twenty years. If you stayed in any Hilton Hotel between 2000 and 2020, you've seen Kristina's work.

Follow the energy. It will take you where you need to go.

Some people find their right path over time. For some of us it's like an epiphany—instant and all at once.

It was like that for my neighbor Rahaf, a content creator and sponsored skateboarder. The first time she rode a skateboard, at the age of twenty-six, she knew she'd found her calling because "All time and space collapsed." She was completely and totally absorbed by the present moment and wanted to stay immersed in that activity. She went on to create a multi-faceted career that grew out of that main love. You'll hear more of her story in Part Three.

That's how it can happen.

A day in our life that changes us forever. That's how it happened for me. . . .

. . . .The day began like any other. But by the time I went to bed that night I was a different person, and forever would be.

There were three of us high school girls stuffed in the back seat of our drama teacher's old Toyota.

We were on our way downtown to a taping of the local TV morning talk show. The TV show had agreed to let us do a 30-second promo to advertise our school play.

Little did I know that those thirty seconds would chart the course for the rest of my life.

As we entered the studio the excitement in the air was palpable, the energy electric. The little hairs on my arms stood up. I wasn't exactly sure what was going to happen, but it felt like *something*. And it was all so *interesting* to me: the fine choreography of the camera people and stage hands and lighting and sound technicians; the hosts, who, I assumed, only worked for that one hour of taping and then went home to read books all day to prep for the next day's interviews. *How cool*, I thought. *What a great way to make a living!*

When the moment came, I took my place under the lights, did my thirty second spiel, and went out to applause. That was it. I was hooked. I'd found my happy place.

High school seemed unbearably mundane after that. But it didn't matter. I knew what I wanted from my life now. I'd had a glimpse into my future, an awareness of a more sparkly world that was mine for the taking.

I think this was the first time it occurred to me that I didn't have to have an ordinary job.

I feel lucky to have found my path, to have that epiphany that working in TV was what I wanted to do with my life, at the age of fifteen. It happened because I *followed the energy.* I loved acting in the plays. Acting in the plays took me to the local TV studio. That took me to Hollywood. The rest is history.

Performing in plays was hands down the best part of my high school experience. I didn't know WHY I loved it and I didn't have to—and that's important: Don't overanalyze joy. Just follow it.

What do *you* live for? What do you geek out about? When do you forget your problems? Meaning, when are you so immersed in the moment, so totally absorbed in what you are doing that, as Rahaf puts it, "Time collapses"? For me, directing and producing can be like that. When I'm collaborating with other creatives, I feel so, so happy, like I did when I was in those high school productions. When I'm in the zone, it's all-consuming and I am totally present. Directing (especially multi-camera) requires 100% concentration and uses a number of my skills at once. My mundane concerns cease to exist. And hours spent that way are extremely satisfying.

Athletes and experts call this the flow state. What activity generates it for you?

I remember the first time I produced a big shoot in New York City, when I was twenty-five. The high it gave me felt incredible. The shoot went very well, and it further confirmed to me that I was made for this role. I came home and told my best friend "I would do this even if no one was paying me." And that was the absolute truth. That's how you should feel.

Now, it's important to note that not in EVERY moment of the process did I feel that way. No. The cameraman had a hissy fit on the location scout. The director was frazzled and going into overtime (which, in television, means in excess of ten or twelve hours in a day). There is stress and risk inherent in complex productions. Not to mention the tedious wrap time, paying invoices, the uncomfortable flights packed into coach like sardines in a can. Not that fun. But when we're rolling—I thrive.

When are you totally happy and engaged?

FOLLOW THE ENERGY, BUT DON'T BE TOO LITERAL

Say you LOVE singing in your church choir. You are totally happy and present-moment in those two hours. Your problems and your "To Do" list cease to exist. But here's an important point: It doesn't mean you need to *sing in a choir* for your living. Or even sing. Just keep doing it. Why? Because it's a clue. There's *something about that* that you love, and it will lead you to your right lane.

Don't judge it. Just go with it. *Follow the energy.*

Here's an example: I love sparkly things. Sequins, rhinestones, disco balls—all of it. I keep small disco ball Christmas tree ornaments on my bedroom window sill, year-round. When the sun floods my bedroom in the morning and hits those little mirrored squares—Oh,

WOW! It blasts polka dots of light all over my walls and ceiling in a random and utterly beautiful fashion. I LOVE the effect SO MUCH! It makes me feel cheerful and happy.

It was, in part, my love of sparkly things that led me to create a line of clothing and sell it to the US Military, thereby financing my next foreign vacation.

And one of my aesthetics I use when I direct on-camera interviews is to manipulate the diopters in the television camera, which has to do with the refractive power of the lens to produce small dots of light on the surfaces of reflective objects out of focus in the background of the shot. Ahhhhh— it looks so pretty. Gives me such pleasure to create that in the shot.

And you know, as a director (or a fashion designer, for that matter) I'm PAID for my aesthetic sensibility.

In the case of my fashion designs, I was initially just *happy* while applying sparkly rhinestones to fabric. It simply made me feel good. And then people paid me for what I designed. My sparkly shirts sold in gyms, hair salons, and on military bases. And that felt good too.

On the set, I'm happy when I'm painting with light and creating pretty pictures that way. And now I've made my living at it for decades. I'm oversimplifying directing here; of course there's more to it than that. But you get the point: Small, seemingly insignificant things that make you happy are clues to what you can wind up doing professionally that will give you joy.

Other kinds of clues I've discovered:

I love working with men. And, in case you didn't know, production crews are (still) mostly men. Some people love being with kids. Or animals. More than with their adult contemporaries. That's a clue.

How do you spend your free time? When you go to a bookstore to browse, what section do you check out first? What section of the newspaper do you reach for first? For me, it was always the pink section of the *San Francisco Examiner*, because that was the arts and entertainment section. What about when you browse online? What are you drawn to? What chance would you JUMP at right now, if given the opportunity?

If you had to blow a thousand dollars in the next ten minutes, what would you blow it on? That can be a clue. (Unless it's coke and whores, in which case, this may not be the book for you.)

What are your obsessions? What can you chat about for hours?

What environments do you like to be in? A quiet, air-conditioned office? The open road? Outdoors under the trees? An art or a dance studio? Your familiar home...or places you've never been? There are no wrong answers.

I once thought about producing in-house corporate videos for hospitals. Healthcare and tech are the industries with the most growth, so it made sense. It was a very left-brain, rational thought. But I couldn't imagine going to work in a hospital every day. I know myself, and I know that being confronted with illness and suffering on a daily basis would be destructive for someone as deep-feeling and emotional as me. (An artist, perhaps? Lol!) But that's me. You may want to work in a hospital, charged by the energy of healing and psyched to play a role in a worthy place, easing people's pain. Cool. *Thank God* for people like you!

You do you, boo, and I'll make sure there's a cool TV show for you to watch at the end of your shift, when you just want to put your feet up and disappear into *Grey's Anatomy*.

So—ENVIRONMENT is key.

Are you climate-sensitive?

I am.

Long ago I decided that if my two choices in life were somehow limited to being a waitress in Key West or a TV producer in Chicago, I'd have to choose the waitress job. But I'm super weather-oriented. Not everyone is. What's important to you?

Initially my love of high school theater made me think I had to be an actress. Later I thought being a TV news anchorwoman would be the bomb. With time comes clarity, and I realized in my twenties that if I worked mired in the negativity that is local TV news, I'd be terribly depressed and probably stressed out. Thank God I figured *that* out. But it was *the community of artists creatively collaborating on the same project* backstage and onstage that FED me. That's what I realized I loved, and working on a television production delivers that for me.

My pal Crystal, a fine artist and muralist you'll read more about throughout this book, put it elegantly: You have to find *THE THING about the thing* that you love!

I never initially set out to work in documentary-style television. I followed the energy and I've made a thirty-year career at it. Who knew the genre was going to blow up like it did? But you know what I DID know? I knew I liked true stories. How? Because I always read nonfiction. Because I like documentaries more than feature films. Because I find

"real" people generally more fascinating than fictional characters. Clues, clues, everywhere!

Just keep turning toward what you love and away from
what you loathe.

Tattoo artist Leonidis, aka Yoshy, makes her art in
Cholula, Mexico. She always loved to draw and followed the
energy to study graphic design. "But it was all about computers, and I *hated* computers!" When she pivoted to becoming
a tattoo artist (more on this later), she discovered she *loved* it.
"That's all I wanted to do: Tattoo. Tattoo, tattoo, tattoo, every
day. I didn't even want days off. I didn't show up for birth-
days, or family reunions, or even church. I worked every day.
I *loved* it."

You ever notice how, when you have to do the dishes or
pay your bills, you're just so *tired*? And then your friends
text because they have an extra ticket to a concert across
town, and all of a sudden you have so much *energy*? We have
energy for the things we love, the things that whisper in our
hearts. Find it, follow it, and use it. It will not let you down.

THERE'S A JOB, AND THEN THERE'S YOUR WORK

To be sure, I've had awful jobs and I've had great jobs, but
the WORK itself I've always loved. And isn't that the best
any of us can hope for?

The distinction I'm drawing between "job" and "work"
is this: I might be on a particular project with a bad boss, an
awful, unrealistic schedule, and a poor budget. That is a
lousy INDIVIDUAL JOB. But the WORK of directing and
producing, that is something I love.

Know too that it's okay to analyze what you *don't* like, and why you don't like it. But, for the love of God, don't analyze what you love. Don't break down joy. It doesn't work like that. Analyzing is a critical and destructive process, and we do not want to do that to the things we love. WHY you love what you love is not important. It's VALID and it's WORTHY and do not question it. Trust it. It's where your genius lies. I promise.

"FAITH, HOPE, AND LOVE, AND THE GREATEST OF THESE IS LOVE"

For me this means the energy of love is the most powerful force there is. Doing what you love is the most powerful action you can take because you have the force of the universe behind you.

Spotlight: John Riesen
The Singing Baseball Player

THE PATH of an opera singer is not something I knew much about. And then I met one on an airplane.

John Riesen, age thirty-two, was flying home to his wife and baby in Buffalo, NY from LA, where he appeared on the television show "America's Got Talent" in a segment that showcased how AI can make even Simon Cowell an opera singer. I'd never met a professional opera singer and I was curious to learn how one makes a living in such a rarified world.

His path struck me as not at all typical, at least in the beginning.

You see, John was on the path to becoming a major league baseball player.

Now, I'm sure a lot of kids have that dream, but not a lot are like John. Turns out he possessed an extraordinary pitching speed. The typical major league player's pitch is ninety to ninety-five mph. John's was eighty-five. At the age of seventeen. So his was not some pipe dream, this was a real possibility for him.

John had supportive parents who were willing to give up their weekends to drive him to games all over Michigan, where he grew up. But if they were going to invest in John's dreams like that, they wanted something in return.

"My dad said, 'To take your talents to the level required to be pro, you're going to have to practice daily. And you have to keep up your grades too. So during the week, your afternoons will be taken up with practice, and your nights with homework. You can see your friends on Saturday nights and Sundays." John agreed to the boundaries. And he worked. Diligently.

He got his pitch up to ninety miles an hour. At eighteen, he was quite possibly on his way to the major leagues.

And then—he took a singing class.

"I discovered I liked it. It takes a lot of training to master your breath, but I had already mastered that as an athlete."

Like Yoshy, the tattoo artist, John said, "Once I could sing, I wanted to sing all the time."

Turns out John is an extraordinarily talented individual, and he was good at singing too. So good, in fact, that his teacher told him, "I think you can go all the way with this and become an opera singer. That's something very few people can do."

John and his parents were blown away. "We were not opera-going folk. I think all I knew about opera was what I knew from Bugs Bunny."

But the time demands of training as an opera singer and the time demands of training for the majors could not peace-fully co-exist. "I had to make a choice. But I was having issues making it. I thought I could be the singing baseball player."

John had come to a fork in the road—and he wanted to go in both directions.

Then one day he did a singing gig at a church. He was cranky that morning, because it required him to get up early, it only paid $50, and he felt he didn't sing his best. "I was so ungrateful for the opportunity, initially." After his performance, however, a woman came up to him in tears, moved by his interpretation of the song. She shared that she was a widow and had been contemplating suicide, but this moment spoke to her and she felt the courage to go on living. "It changed my life. That's something I didn't think I'd ever feel with baseball. No one was ever going to be moved to tears by my pitching. I realized what I could do with this gift. Up till then it was just fun. But suddenly, I had meaning behind it."

John threw himself into training as a singer with all the dedication and discipline he had applied as an athlete. "A lot of artists struggle with the sheer discipline it takes—being told 'No' fifteen times out of sixteen; performing when your body isn't working correctly." But John was already skilled at that from baseball. "I had an understanding of failure and loss. Perhaps the hardest part of being an artist is the discipline of handling rejection. You can make it all the way to callbacks, and then you lose."

In fact, just recently John was up for a role in a European tour with a bunch of A-list celebrities from Broadway and the opera world, that he really, really wanted to do. The pay was great, the destinations fabulous, and it fit in well with his family life. "It came down to two of us, and they said I was too old." The other guy was only twenty!

"For a day or two, I was like 'That sucks!' But I know it's not true." John counsels, "Get used to that part of your life."

I asked John if he had any regrets about the path he has chosen, and he said "I would have loved to have seen what would have happened [with baseball]. But it's just so clear to me that I was meant to be a performer." John's "thing about the thing," as Crystal described it, is "communicating and affecting people emotionally." I'm not surprised. He's a great storyteller. I hope you get to sit next to him on an airplane.

Chapter Two

Talents vs. Skills

SKILLS ARE talents developed over time.

What does this mean?

I have a good eye. That's a talent—a gift. Over time, I've developed my eye by shooting for 10,000 hours. (If you're familiar with any of Malcolm Gladwell's books, you know that becoming an expert in anything takes about 10,000 hours.) So now I have the SKILL of knowing how to light and shoot a room, or a person, or a scene (people in a room or landscape). That's a skill. I know how to direct nine cameras at once. That's a skill.

I've always had a facility for language. That's a talent. Being able to write well and fast—that's a skill. Being able to communicate precisely to a cameraman the vision in my head and the expectation of how we create that—that's a skill. And skills are what people pay for. Not talents. Michael Jackson was soooo incredibly talented, it was beyond belief. I watched him rehearse in person one time and I noticed how incredibly facile he was at picking up the choreography. That's a skill. See the difference?

Talents are the gifts we are born with—the things that come easily to us. Skills can be learned and improved upon. We need to develop our skills to be able to express our creative gifts. No matter how talented you are, to be successful you have to learn to master your craft. It takes time. And practice. And it's oh-so-worth it to deliver you the life of your dreams.

Having a good eye isn't going to make me any money unless I turn it into a skill. Now, don't get me wrong, it HELPS that I have a good eye. But no one's going to hire someone who simply has a good eye. You probably wouldn't hire me to paint a mural, because I haven't developed my eye to use it in mural painting. But you probably wouldn't hire a muralist to direct a TV show. So your talents can take you in different directions, based on how you choose to develop your skills.

I write something just about every day. But writing for a television show is a skill. It's also a craft. I learned how to write for the ear, rather than the page. I learned how to write to picture. I learned how to write well and fast, because TV always has tight, immovable deadlines. Writing for TV is a skill.

I converse easily with anyone. I'm not shy, and I like people. But disarming them, or gaining their trust and confidence quickly—skill. An important one, in my line of work, and one I have been told, on more than one occasion, that I've been hired because of. (Now, a con artist probably has developed this same skill, so again, you can take a talent and turn it into a number of different skills that take you in different directions!)

Yoshy, the tattoo artist mentioned earlier, knew she wanted to be an artist because she was always drawing. Turning that raw talent into the skill of tattooing was something she had to learn over time. She practiced on herself and her friends for two months when she first bought the equipment. Then she got a job in a studio, doing small tattoos for a year. Now she's been making her living at it for seventeen years and has opened her own studio in Mexico.

If you are a person with a lot of talents (and, dear reader, I believe you are, if you were drawn to this book), you will need to choose which skill sets to develop your talents into. And I realize it can be difficult to pick amongst the many glittering options this world offers you. So a final word about picking something: You MUST. You simply have to.

Don't worry about making a wrong choice. Nothing you do early in your career will go to waste. You develop your skills through experience, and you will be learning no matter what you pick to get started. You will use everything you learn, one way or another.

Picking a direction is really important. We all know any number of talented, smart people who are frozen, and living nowhere close to their potential. Doesn't it make you sad? You don't want to be that person. I really appreciate how smart, talented people can fall into this trap because there are so many things they CAN do. But life is short, dear ones, and you can't afford to be stagnant, spinning your wheels on idle. Pick something. And expect to course-correct. Because you WILL. And that's GOOD. And you SHOULD.

What do I mean by course-correcting?

Here's an illustration:

When a pilot gets in the cockpit, he or she has a destination in mind. But from what I understand about aerodynamics—which, admittedly, isn't much—they actually don't fly in a straight line. The weather conditions and wind dynamics all play a part in that pilot continually HAVING TO REDIRECT. Fly higher or lower, faster or slower, to avoid a weather system or a pocket of turbulence or a strong headwind. They NAVIGATE based on new information they are acquiring with incoming data. They still get to their destination, but as they gain more knowledge of conditions along the route, they adjust accordingly. I just love this analogy.

Ideally, as you move through your journey, trying new things and learning about yourself, you will grow, and you will be in a better position to make bigger decisions.

Kim, a graphic artist in Arizona, initially studied Pre-Med at the University of Iowa. The two career paths are not as divergent as you might think. Kim says both science and art require you to "think broadly and deeply, be very curious, and be happy to work alone." But she had the heart of an artist, and by that I mean she *listened* to what her heart was telling her: She longed to be a visual artist. "That voice, that force we can't deny in us, that drives us to be authentic. That's what makes us an artist. It's not the work." She followed the energy and studied fine art.

If you're a full-fledged adult reading this, and maybe aren't "where you wanted to be at thirty," for example, I think it's important to realize that you don't have to be 100% loyal to that sixteen-year-old you were who wanted X. Because that sixteen-year-old, God love her, didn't know as much as YOU do now. She had a really limited set of data to draw on. No thirty-year-old in their right mind would trust their big life decisions to a sixteen-year-old, now would they? That would be insane. So don't fall into that trap of feeling like a failure because your life doesn't look like what the teen you or the child you thought it should by now. Have a little chat with your inner child if you must and tell her, "You had GREAT ideas. And I'm glad. But now you have a responsible adult to helm the ship for you, so you need to trust that she's acting in your best interests."

It can be overwhelming to decide what to do with your life, especially when you are young. Don't. Just do what feels right for you right now. As Rumi said, "As you start to walk on your way, the path appears."

Spotlight: Heather Horton
Comedian/Actor

HEATHER HORTON IS an actor and stand-up comic I worked with on *Last Comic Standing*. Her creative dreams took her from a small town in South Carolina (Anderson, population 30,000) to being a working actress in Hollywood. You've seen her on television shows such as *Parks and Recreation* and *The Orville*.

Heather's life is a prime example of following the energy. She's an extremely physical person, who always loved dancing and playing soccer. In high school, she won both a dance school scholarship and a collegiate athletic scholarship. She also always loved school and studying. Paying attention to all these things she loved, and DOING them, led her to a kind of a la carte life that works for her, physically, emotionally, and financially.

When I met Heather, she was doing stand-up in Nashville and working as a physical therapist, her first career. As a kid, she had no idea she would be an actress. "Growing up, physical therapists would come into the dance school and do injury screening." That looked like a cool job she could see herself doing. But she wasn't able to get into PT school in South Carolina. "I tanked on my interviews. So I applied to school in Nashville and was accepted." Although Heather already had a bachelor's degree in biology, she found PT school to be very demanding. "It was hard. You have to take gross anatomy, just like the doctors do, and if you don't pass, you're done."

Heather began to feel consumed by the rigors of school. "I started missing life as an athlete, missing dance, missing all these things I loved." So she followed the energy and incorporated those things back into her life. She joined a soccer team that played on the weekends, and she started ballroom dancing. She never imagined these things would lead her to Hollywood. But that's how following the energy works.

The soccer coach on her weekend team noticed how funny she was and suggested she become an actor. "I said, 'No, I'm not an actor.'" But the coach and some players on her team went to a local comedy club for a show, and Heather was intrigued. The club gave a stand-up class and Heather signed up. Not surprisingly, she found it to be a lot of fun.

Her coach wrote a short film that featured Heather. "I just loved the process of it. We recorded voiceover at his house and filmed at my condo. I thought I should start taking classes."

By this time, Heather was a practicing PT, taking stand-up classes and improv and developing her skills. She also started acting in productions at local film schools. "I did twelve films in twelve months." In one of these productions, she was given the title role. "I was in, like, every scene. I took my two weeks of vacation from my PT job so that I could do it." The film school held a screening of the film. The theater was packed to a sold-out crowd. "I was so nervous, I only took two friends. I sat all scrunched down in the seat." The film was a hit. And Heather got noticed. She received the best actress award at the festival. "People came up and talked to me after. That's when I thought 'Maybe I can make a living doing this.'"

She was also feeling that maybe the south wasn't exactly the right place for her. "Growing up in a small town, I just always felt there was something bigger for me." If she was going to pursue acting seriously, she needed to move.

"My mom would always say, 'I wish I had gone to New York and been a Rockette.'" Heather didn't want to have similar regrets later in life. "But I'm not 'Broadway.' My strength was comedy, and I felt like I was more 'TV.'" And the place for TV was Hollywood. "It's easier to follow the energy when you're younger. We get taught to censor ourselves." Planning a life in Los Angeles, from Nashville, however, was not without its issues.

"Every time you looked for an apartment or work [online] it was just so scammy. I thought 'I just have to get there,'" get boots on the ground to assess the situation.

She lined up a roommate she knew from Nashville. She figured she'd give herself three months in LA to get situated. The PT job she found required a long commute to Compton, and while riding the Metro, Heather would read acting books, find out which theaters were close, and research where the good improv and scene study classes were and what the best places were for stand-up. She knew that her goal was to switch to part-time PT work, or at the very least, do a PT job where she could make her own schedule to accommodate auditions.

In line at Costco one day, a man noticed her scrubs and recruited her to work for a different PT agency, one that would allow more flexibility. The pieces of the puzzle were starting to fit together. The new role allowed her to make her own schedule and essentiality be her own boss. "It was very unsteady. I got better at budgeting."

The first time she felt like she'd really made it when she co-starred on *Parks and Recreation*. "I don't know how I got into that room. Amy Poehler was on the other side of the glass. I'm sitting there with Aziz Ansari, and I'm like—!! No one prepares you for that!"

Heather still believes working on student films is a great way to keep your chops up and learn the business. "I never think I'm too big for that." I pointed out to her that that's also an excellent way to network, because you are meeting future filmmakers and industry professionals. "I didn't even think of it that way. I was just thinking about learning how to be on set."

Now, as a self-described "recovering workaholic" who previously did some sort of acting-related class or performance every night of the week, she emphasizes the importance of having a balanced life that will make you happy. "I've learned over the years to have other things outside the industry [that you enjoy doing] and I've had to *learn* this. All those fun things about you that make you unique as a character—have fun doing the things you need to do."

Chapter Three

Producing Your Life 101: The Board

INTRODUCING: THE BOARD

OKAY, so let's say you're following the energy, have found the clues, and you think you know exactly what creative career you want. Great!

Do you know exactly how to get there? It can be difficult for creatives to know precisely what steps to take to advance our careers. It's not like being a lawyer. There's no set protocol of "major in politics, go to law school, graduate, intern, pass the Bar," and voila, you're a lawyer. It might be a whole lot easier if there was a simple, prescriptive path to follow.

When I was coming up, I wanted a tool to help me get where I wanted to be, in my career and in life. So I created one by adapting techniques I was learning producing TV shows to *produce my life.*

Producers bring a big, complicated, creative project into

existence. We take an idea, craft it into a vision, and make it
into reality. We produce results you can *see*.

As a supervising producer and director, I have a finite
number of scenes to tell a story, and a precise, allotted
screen time—44 minutes for a one-hour show and 22 for a
half-hour show—*to tell the whole story.* (Commercials have
even less!) What scenes am I going to put in what order to
tell the story most effectively? Where are the act breaks
going to land? There are a lot of decisions to be made, and
limited time and money. (Does that sound anything like
your life?)

What if I told you that there's a simple *physical tool*
producers use that you can recreate to help you produce
your life?

YOUR PERSONAL PRODUCTION BOARD

Inside every television production office you will see the
same thing: a Production Board. It's the visual checklist of
what needs to be shot, and in what order. Its physical
construction is rudimentary. It's usually a cork bulletin
board, maybe 2' by 3', mounted on a wall. On that board are
columns of index cards. The Board is simple, but magical in
its effectiveness. We use it because it works. And has, for
decades. There's a Board (we literally refer to it as "The
Board") in every Supervising Producer's office I've ever been
in or inhabited. If you look carefully, you'll see it often on
TV shows when they go behind-the-scenes and film a
segment in their production office. (Late Night shows, especially, do this a lot. I notice it on *Saturday Night Live* all the
time when they go behind-the-scenes in the office. You'll

notice a list of what comedic segments or "bits" are in each act of the show.)

Your next step will be to create a Personal Production Board. And before you object to using a physical board, see below for "Why You Must Do This the Analog Way." Not on your phone or tablet. You'll need to use physical index cards, pushpins, and a cork board. Why? BECAUSE IT WORKS. So bear with me here.

A television production, like any big production, is complex. There's the budget, the schedule, the cast, the crew...dozens of people to be hired, supervised, motivated, managed, and coordinated. There are vendors up and down; permits from the city to be obtained; props and vehicles to be bought or rented; deals to be made; and on and on. There's a lot of money at stake, and people tend to get stressed about that. But the whole reason we went into TV was to do something fun and creative. So: how to integrate all the necessary moving parts and accomplish a ton in a short period of time?

When you have a Herculean project to accomplish, your only chance is to eat the elephant one bite at a time: to break it down into smaller steps. This, I know, is not new to you. What MAY be new to you is that as producers, we have learned how to do this visually, and it's kinda brilliant. Because we are visually-oriented people. I mean, we take words on a page and translate them into PICTURES. That's what we excel at.

Remember when you studied for tests in school? And you highlighted passages in actual textbooks? Maybe you even wrote notes in the margins. Didn't that help you with recall when test time came? Couldn't you sometimes picture the exact page in the book where your yellow highlighted paragraph was? Your memory flashed back to those high-lighted bits, those visual reminders of what was important to you.

The Board works the same way.

For example: As a field producer (the producer who actually goes on set, in the field, to get the story shot), I'd get an outline (like a script) on my desk of the story I was to produce. At this point, the TV show only exists on paper. The first thing I would do is read it once through, without stopping, to understand the story. I wanted to get the over-view of the whole story and let it affect me emotionally. Was this a mystery? A love story? An action story with lots of stunts? And most importantly: What grabbed me emotion-ally? What stood out? Because that would be the core of the story and the reason for producing it.

The parallel to your life is this: What do you WANT? What makes you excited? What grabs your attention? Because *that* is what is worth producing in your life. What dreams are you trying to bring into the world?

In my case, I wanted loving relationships, meaningful work, and travel, in that order. I knew this, in part, because I journaled regularly to clarify what I wanted out of life. (A journal is an excellent companion to your Personal Produc-tion Board.) These became my top three life goals. Secondary goals included having friends who had the time and the money with whom to travel the world, and becoming a tennis player. This is what my twenty-five-year-old self's Board reflected.

How you write your story is up to you. What this tool does is take your story from the amorphous dream state into reality. It lets you produce the movie that is your life.

My life at forty looked very much like the life I set out to produce when I was twenty-five, and that is no accident. Using The Board was the one tool, more than any other, that got me the life I envisioned for myself. I also credit it with getting me promoted to being the youngest producer on a hit TV show when I was twenty-five.

As mentioned in Chapter Two, your goals can and will and SHOULD change over time. Doesn't matter. That's the beauty of this tool. You're going to change it to suit your changing needs. It can serve you for the rest of your life. It works as well for a twenty-year-old as a forty-year-old.

USING THE PRODUCTION BOARD TO PRODUCE YOUR LIFE

I pinned on The Board, on white index cards, the big categories of what I wanted to produce in my life: TRAVEL, PRODUCER, SOCIAL, TENNIS, etc. (Just like the various acts that make up a TV show.)

Every Sunday, I'd write in my journal about what I wanted and what I could do THAT week to get closer to my intended goals. For example: I could practice tennis. I could approach a producer I admired and ask to sit in on her casting session or budget meetings so I could learn what those were like. After I noodled in my journal about what was going on at the office that week and what I could do, practically, to take advantage of those goings-on, I had a number of ideas. I'd write those ideas (tasks) on colored index cards (with the colors chosen at random). There were concrete things, such as practice 100 serves, and more amorphous ones such as "Position yourself in the Executive

Producers' minds as the next logical choice to be promoted."

Needless to say, these amorphous steps were a little trickier than something concrete like "practice 100 serves." But they have their place on your Board too, because you will SEE them regularly. They will stick in your mind, and then when something comes up that will advance you toward the task, you'll be hyper-aware when that opportunity presents itself and in a better position to take advantage of it.

Keep your Board someplace where you can see it every day. I kept mine propped up on my bedroom floor, against the wall. That way, it was the first thing I glanced at every morning before I got out of bed.

Judging by the popularity of vision boards in recent decades, we know that this stuff works. Pictures are memorable. So are colors. I believe the colors work on your subconscious. Somehow, the colors help you recall the card, which helps you recall the specific task, which is useful when you are out in the world, spotting opportunities that will further your goals.

I know vision boards are powerful. But a Personal Production Board allows you to see the various *concrete* steps that you need to take to get you where you want to go. And unlike a vision board, which is usually created and then hung up, unchanging, until you have achieved those goals for yourself, a Production Board is dynamic. It changes often—every week, in fact, as you complete certain tasks and new goals arise.

And things change. Your Board, like your life, is dynamic. The network calls and wants *this* now instead of *that*. The main location we wanted isn't available for filming that day, etc. This is why we use the cards—so simple and easy to move. And move them you will—especially when you accomplish your tasks one by one, every week, and remove those cards to make room for your next set of tasks.

After you have assembled your Board, step back and take a look at it. Which of these things can you accomplish this week? Get out your phone and schedule those things into your calendar for the week. Want to practice serves? Book a court for when you are free on Sunday. Want to connect with fellow adventurers and have buddies to travel with? Text that pal for a drink on Friday night to further that relationship. If you do this every week, you'll be AMAZED at how fast it works.

CONSISTENCY IS KEY

Work on your Board once a week, every week. The next Sunday, review your Board, take off the cards for the things you've accomplished, and put up new cards for the new ideas you have from noodling in your journal. I recommend keeping the cards, because it is kind of amazing to look back at the stack of them and all the things you have accomplished that are moving you towards your goals.

It's like being on a hike. Have you ever reached a vista point, then looked back and you CAN'T BELIEVE HOW FAR YOU'VE COME? This happens to me on the hiking trail all the time. Using The Board, it will happen in much the same way.

WHY YOU MUST DO IT THE ANALOG WAY

I understand that digital is *everything*. I get that being away from your phone is like losing a limb. I get it.

But in television we do this on a PHYSICAL, ANALOG BOARD WITH INDEX CARDS. Why?

BECAUSE IT WORKS. Really frickin' well.

Studies have shown that the more senses you employ while reading, the better you remember the content. You TOUCH the index cards. You WRITE on them. You PUSH the pushpins through them into the cork. The COLORS help you recall the card. The non-uniformity of your personal handwriting sticks in your brain better than typed text. It just does. It will resonate with you in a different way, I promise.

Everything else you do is on the flat, two-dimensional screen—your phone, your tablet, your laptop. Let this be the one thing that is not.

Use your phone for your calendar if you want. Use your tablet or laptop for journaling if you must. Record your ideas on your phone if you're so inclined. But I implore you to use the actual Board the analog way. **In TV we still do it this way, because we know its power.** We PRODUCE results. A show. We bring it into being. We bring IDEAS into REALITY. We take the AMORPHOUS and make it concrete. And we only have time for a tried-and-true system that works.

You know how a To Do List can feel annoying? And overwhelming? Somehow The Board never does. Maybe it's because I confine it to things that are going to further my goals, and looking at the progress I'm making towards my goals brings me joy and peace.

Maybe The (analog) Board works so effectively because it tickles your RAS: the Reticulated Activating System. It's a part of your brain stem that bridges your subconscious and conscious self; the part of your brain used to manifest what your heart desires. I'm no neuroscientist, so someone else out there can explain the energetic transfer better than me, but I know The Board is powerful. I'm convinced The Board interacts with the RAS.

To see photos of my Boards and those of colleagues, find me on the socials or Jeannie-ONeill.com. I'd love to see photos of yours too. Let's create a community of like-minded creatives who support each other. And you can see what big goals I'm working on lately!

Spotlight: Tammy Horton
Photographer/Accidental Business Owner

"I ACCIDENTALLY WOUND UP WITH A BUSINESS," says my colleague, Tammy, a stills photographer (no relation to Heather Horton).

"I grew up in North Carolina, the first one of my family to go to college. I always wanted to do something creative. I was interested in photography and filmmaking, but everyone said there's no money in that, so I went to Florida and studied marine biology. I was living someone one else's life."

Tammy course-corrected (literally and figuratively) and transferred to Tennessee to study at UT. She initially studied graphic design there "because I thought graphic designers make money." But after taking a really interesting photography class, she course-corrected again and switched her major to film, photography, and video.

The summer before her senior year, she and a friend moved to LA "with no plan. We just drove till we hit the beach. Then we kind of thought 'now what'?" She called a professor mentor in Tennessee, who had a friend who was a director on *The Drew Carey Show*. He allowed them to stay with him for two weeks.

"We were going out all the time and meeting people. Photography was always in the back of my head, but I was scared to pursue it. We met a couple of young guys who worked in TV and let us couch surf for the rest of the summer. It was a total bachelor pad. We kept our clothes in the kitchen cabinets because they didn't have any food in them. We met the comic, Theo Von, who was on *Road Rules*, and he became our friend. That's the way LA works. Stuff will happen for you. There're so many people there following that energy and that dream, you're going to overlap."

Tammy and I overlapped on a television show I was directing on at the time. Tammy was a production assistant and psyched to be making "$400 a week *PLUS MILEAGE—WOO-HOO!*" In that environment she was occasionally given the opportunity to shoot stills for the show. "I think I shot skateboarders and a chimpanzee," because the producers knew of her interest in photography and supported her.

Some years later, another show that both she and I were working on ended and, after filing for unemployment, she wondered, *Now what?* "I thought, 'Well, TV is over right now, so what's next?'"

She answered an ad on Craigslist for an associate wedding photographer in Long Beach. "The stuff this photographer who ran the ad posted was so different—it was artsy and moody and not like typical wedding photographs at all. It piqued my curiosity."

The woman asked Tammy to send some photos she'd

shot. Tammy did not feel she was entirely ready. Everything wasn't perfect. She had a crappy camera, no portfolio, or even any wedding photos to send.

But she trusted the universe and acted. She followed the energy.

She sent along three artsy photos she had taken of a friend doing yoga poses, telling the photographer, "'Well, here's what my eye is like.'" Then they met up in person and hit it off. "She saw something in me and was even willing to rent me a better camera for shoots." The woman hired her as a part-time associate photographer, promising her 30% of the cut from the jobs they booked. Tammy was over the moon. "I was like 'You're gonna pay me HOW much *to shoot a wedding?*'" It was almost double what she had been making as a script supervisor in television production.

She photographed her first wedding and *loved* it. "I felt like such an imposter because I was like 'This is so fun and easy.'"

Tammy went on to shoot under the woman for another couple of years and, increasingly, for weddings of friends and connections who would solicit her. "The business accidentally happened and just snow-balled. It wasn't until I made my move to Northern California that I put some effort into it."

Like many young artists, Tammy soon found herself at a crossroads personally and professionally. "Everyone at the age I was, they were all into their next transition, which was basically getting married and having kids, and I was like, 'Okay, what's my next transition, if it's not that?'" [I really relate to this. I was in my early thirties when I transitioned from being a producer into being a director and then a multi-camera director.]

Tammy moved to a small town in Northern California, where she could feel closer to nature. "Northern California changed my career as far as what I've been able to shoot up here—the redwoods, cliffs, beaches. We have such great access to nature. It changed my style and approach. People are more chill up here. We're outside more than in LA. The energy is different."

As Tammy's artistic style developed in relationship to the new environment, so did her clientele.

Since she didn't have the connections in Northern California that she had from years of living in Southern California, she had to put on her big girl panties and level up her business. "I moved up here and thought "'Well, I guess I better get a business license!'"

Tammy says the money she invested in her business paid off tremendously.

"Once I started putting money into my business, I saw the returns double. I got a Covid grant and paid $6,000 to upgrade my website, which was totally worth it. It changed my bookings and the type of client that reaches out to me. I hired someone for $500 a month to increase my social media presence and found I got a lot more engagement and inquiries."

It's been fun to watch Tammy evolve over the years, both in her artistic style and in her business.

"I just realized I'm providing a service, and I noticed things shifted when I focused on *that*: taking care of the clients during their special occasion. They're going to be happy with the photos, that's a given." [See how she's grown from her younger self, who "felt like an imposter," into a working artist of twenty years who is totally confident in the quality of the art she makes? I love to see this. And it reminds me of my content creator/skateboarder neighbor, Rahaf, saying, "Borrow some confidence from your future self."] Now Tammy has clients tell her all the time "'You make it so easy and enjoyable,'" and she says that's where the magic is. "That's when I get all the referrals."

Tammy found her niche as a photographer. She loves that she's there for people on a special day for them. "Shooting models is so fleeting. But the photos I'm taking are going to mean something to people who aren't even born yet. Sometimes I've shot someone who's now passed on, and the family uses the photo I took as their obituary photo." She loves that her art is significant in that way.

Tammy's story illustrates a lot of what we've talked about thus far: Following the energy, and course-correcting. How you may not feel like you are totally ready, and that's perfectly okay. Don't let that stop you from moving forward on your dream. And how environment can be key to your success, both in terms of who you bump up against, but also how your art is influenced and evolves.

You may know, or have at least seen a wedding photographer or two, where you live. That particular career doesn't seem so far out of reach, does it? And yet, Tammy tells us how even *that* felt scary to her because of all the stories she grew up with about how "You can't make a living being a photographer." She's been proving the naysayers wrong for twenty years now.

Part Two

Let's Get This Show On The Road

Chapter Four

Find Your Tribe

DISAPPOINTING THE ONES YOU LOVE

ONCE UPON A TIME I was a field producer/director on the NBC show *Last Comic Standing*. It was lots of fun, and I adored working with the comics. They were wonderfully collaborative and hard-working, and creating bits with them in the field was super gratifying.

I interviewed dozens of comics over the course of many months, and a frequent question I liked to ask them was, "What did your parents say when you told them you were going to be a stand-up comic for a living?"

Please understand—I am not maligning comedians in any way. I think you *get* my philosophy enough by now to know that I think being a comic is a perfectly legitimate career path.

But not everyone agrees with me. In fact, I *started* asking that question because so many of the talented performers I was working with had told me stories, on and off camera, about how they were in grad school, or in one case, *medical school* when they decided to change their career trajectories and pursue making strangers laugh for a living.

One of the comics was from India and explained to me that there actually was no tradition of even *being* a stand-up comic in India, so his parents were terribly confused by his choices.

Why am I telling you these stories?

Because I think it's important for you to get comfortable with the idea that pursuing your creative dreams might not sit well with everyone you love. Specifically, if you are young and just starting out: your parents. The ones who raised you and fed you and wiped your butt, and maybe, if you were extra lucky, even paid for your education. And you are grateful. No one wants to disappoint those they love. But it happens. And adulting means getting comfortable with that fact.

Maybe you have open-minded parents who are less concerned about you making money than they are about you being creatively fulfilled and happy. And if so, bully for you. But sometimes there's a price to pay when it comes to your relationships.

I've read that the famous singer/songwriter/actor and Grammy winner Kris Kristofferson was rejected by his parents when he took his Rhodes-Scholar-Oxford-educated-Army-officer-butt down to Nashville to become a star. (I wonder if any part of John Legend's dad still wishes John had a "normal" career.)

Even if you don't become famous, it's worth noting that a lot of us with creative careers still feel what my friend Allan, an audio engineer, meant when he said, "My parents still don't know exactly what it is I do." That can be a bummer.

And here's another news flash: As you get older, and other relationships become more central to your life, not every romantic partner you ever have may be totally on-board with these life-outside-the-box career goals of yours. It happens.

My hope is that you have parents and loved ones who truly want the best for you, even if it clashes with their ideas of preferred careers for you.

But if you don't, the best way I know to counterbalance the pain that comes with that is to surround yourself with others who support your desires and are also on *their* unique paths. In other words: Find Your Tribe.

FINDING YOUR TRIBE

Being a creative—which, by definition, is someone who sees things differently from most people—can be both a lonely and a long path.

It's imperative you surround yourself with like-minded people.

This may mean you have to move. Your butt, yes, but the city you live in may have to change too.

I grew up in San Francisco. Right in the city. And yes, the city was full of creative people living nontraditional lives. (Or at least it was before the tech boom, followed by the explosion of the real estate market and artists moving out because they couldn't afford the rents; but I digress.) And had I been older when I faithfully announced my dream to people, I'm sure I would have been able to find my people.

But as it was, I was only fifteen years old when I decided that I wanted to work in television, and let's just say I wasn't surrounded by people who shared my dream.

More than that, I was actually surprised to find no end of people who were only too happy to s—t on my dream.

When I announced that I wanted to work in TV, with all the optimism of a teen, who believes anything is possible, you'd think I'd just said I wanted to play in the NBA for all the encouragement I got.

"Oh, *everyone* wants to do *that*," they'd say, as if it was totally beyond my reach.

By the time I was seventeen, I hit the road for LA. And a funny thing happened when I got there: When I said I wanted to work in TV, the response was more likely to be "Oh, my next-door neighbor's dad's uncle's dog-sitter is a studio chef!" Or "My aunt used to work on *Jeopardy*." Or "Oh, cool. I'm an actor and personal trainer."

Everyone in LA, it seemed, knew or at least had heard of someone, maybe twice removed, but STILL, who had worked in television. And this gave me hope. Initially. Later on it gave me ideas. And connections. And opportunities. But in the beginning, hope was enough. Everyone agreed this career path was possible.

Say what you will about LA (although I find it terribly clichéd and tiresome to do so), this is a town where people don't sh— on your dreams. Tell any stranger you just met that you want to be an actress, designer, singing yoga teacher, whatever, and they will probably share with you their own creative dreams and endeavors.

This is a city that attracts dreamers, and while that may mean that maybe everyone isn't making as much money as on Wall St. or in Silicon Valley, it's all right with me. Dreams just don't seem so far out of reach here.

Fulfilling your dream could take a while. Who do you want to be surrounded by during that time? People who think the odds of you achieving your creative potential are about the same as you landing on the moon? Or people who *know* hitting it big is possible because their manicurist knows someone who did. *And* they're working toward their dream right along with you.

I have a friend, Henry. He's a painter. A really good one. He's also gay, sometimes flamboyantly so, and El Salvadoran, and a vegetarian. I met him in LA, natch. And he wound up living, working, and prospering in Houston. TEXAS.

I was shooting there, and we hung out one night with his friends. I just couldn't imagine Henry finding his niche there, in this middle-American, gun-totin', flag-wavin', beef-eatin' town.

But you know what? He has.

This particular night neither one of us had a car.

"Oh, don't worry," Hen said. "My friends Bliss and Sushi will pick us up."

"You have friends named Bliss and Sushi? In *Houston*?"

He did, and they were super cool. Sushi's real name was Susan, but because she was the only remotely Asian (Indonesian, actually) kid the other kids in her school had ever seen, they nick-named her Sushi. Bliss was Pakistani, his real name being Farhad, which in English roughly translates to bliss.

We joined an international and eclectic group of Henry's friends, who were celebrating someone's recent return from Paris. One of the clique was into sailing small boats around the world, and his wife was into some pretty wild escapades herself, but I digress. This was not the crowd I expected to find in the heartland, and I said so to Henry.

"You can find your people anywhere," he said, and there's a good lesson in that.

So maybe you don't have to move cities after all. In my case, it proved extremely helpful.

At the moment, I'm in Starbucks. The tables are jammed so close together that I can tell that to my left is a cartoonist who is reading an art magazine and sketching. To my right is someone who appears to be editing music. And I'll just bet I can't throw a sugar packet without hitting someone who's working on a script.

All I'm saying is, you need support, and if you don't have it among your family of origin, you must make an effort to go out and find it.

"The dancer seeks out a community of dancers wherever they go," says Leymis Bolaños Wilmott, a choreographer I know who strategically chose to found her dance company in Sarasota, Florida. "I could have done it anywhere ... but Sarasota and their support of the arts is unique. I'm not here by accident." But it wasn't an immediate decision. Leymis is Cuban, grew up in Miami, and after promoting clubs on South Beach as a way to earn money to train in New York, she gravitated back to her home state, where she's found her tribe.

Leymis underscores the importance of investing in a community of creative peers. "Enter into that community. Work backstage or intern. That gets noticed."

Her advice reminds me of the extraordinary actor Harry

Belafonte. He fell in love with the theater and got a job cleaning a theater so he could be around actors.

Plus, all creative people, I'm convinced, suffer from that little voice in their head. You know the one. It's the one you hear saying, "This is *dumb*. No one's gonna like this. It is isn't good enough. *You're* not good enough. Whatever gave you the idea anyone would like to look at/see/hear/read/pay money for *this?* This is crap. Hang it up now and go to law school."

You may know this as Imposter Syndrome. Guess what? It never goes away! If you are learning and growing and stretching your creative boundaries farther and wider and higher than you ever have before, this devil on your shoulder is just part and parcel of doing that.

That's when it becomes really helpful to have people around to talk you down from the bridge and maybe even to inspire you by the creative work they're doing.

Nothing significant is achieved in a vacuum. And being a creative isn't *really* as 100% original as you might think. If there's something you want to do, odds are someone else is out there doing it. Go find that person. And others like them. And help each other make your dreams come true.

Chapter Five

On Courage: How to Ask for What You Want

Now that you have an inkling about what you want to do in this world, you are going to have to ask for help. Or at the very least, cooperation—from God, from the Universe, from your parents, your friends, your colleagues, your boss, your spouse, and on and on. Often we are so uncomfortable with this. *Why?* Is it because to be human is to feel undeserving, on some deep level? Because we know we are flawed creatures? I don't know, but it does seem to be a commonality we all struggle with at times. Regardless, the truth of the matter is, you're going to have to ask for things.

Maybe some of you were raised in households that taught you this skill. And good for you if you were. But I'm going to bet a lot of us were raised in households that taught us to be humble. Modest. Unassuming. Not prideful. What's that old saying about the nail that sticks out gets hammered down? And what about being ladylike? Or not letting people know what you are thinking? Saving face. A million societal and cultural instructions that have been put on us to "Go along to get along." To "Be seen and not heard." No wonder so many of us sit passively by and let the rewards we desire go to someone else.

But what about "Ask and you shall receive"?

"Seek and you shall find"?

"Knock and the door shall be opened to you"?

I minored in Political Science (because I wanted to be an anchorwoman at that time and I thought it would be helpful. Turns out I found those classes far more interesting than most of my major's classes, but I digress). A particular professor in that department had a policy that if you didn't like the grade she gave you on a paper, you could go talk to her during office hours and argue your case. Man, I did NOT want to do this. But I also got money for my grades, in terms of scholarships because of my GPA, so those numbers were important to me. So I went in, again and again (I had her for several classes), if I got anything less than an A. It made me SO NERVOUS to do it! I hated it! But you know what? I did it anyway. And you know what else? She raised my grade. EVERY. SINGLE. TIME. Every time, I was glad I did it. The risk and the pain paid off.

Now, as an older adult, I realize that she was rewarding my courageousness at overcoming my fear and doing something that was difficult for me. The paper never changed. But I did. And I took that skill with me into my career and my life. And boy, what an asset it has been.

As travel writer Jill Robinson says, "If you don't ask, you don't get. This stuff is not gonna drop in your lap. You have to hustle."

You HAVE to ask. And you have to believe in the value, the worth, of what you have to contribute. I like this word "contribute." I like it better than "what you have to offer." Because "offer" is so often viewed as a gift—as in a free thing. An offering. But a *contribution* is something else indeed. Something of significant value.

So let's assume you KNOW what you want, both the macro and the micro. (The macro would be "I want a job in television," for example. And the micro would be "I want *this* particular job.) And now you have to ask for it. And you want it soooo badly you can taste it. That strong emotion, that *energy,* can be both good and bad. It can propel you towards your goal, or, if it is perceived as desperate, or needy, or overbearing, it can backfire.

A lot of us get blocked here. All that insecurity and doubt and fear in our heads can stop us from mustering the courage to power through these emotions.

I feel you. I really, really, do.

When I was a novice producer, climbing my way up the ladder on my first major network TV show, I broke out in a red flush on my neck every time I went in to my boss to ask for a raise. Can you imagine? Not only was it embarrassing, I knew it gave me away. So I began to wear a long-sleeved turtleneck sweater into the office every time I went in to ask for a raise. I did. (I've often wondered if my boss ever caught on. If he ever stopped to say to himself, "There she is in that turtleneck again. In JULY. What's it going to cost me this time?" I got the raises, though. In fact, I quadrupled my salary in two years. Does that sound like something you'd like to do?

No lesser a text than *The Bible* says, "Ask and you shall receive." But you have to ask.

I have a tennis buddy who brags about the fact that she's

never asked for a raise. That is insane to me. I don't know what she makes, but I guarantee you she is underpaid. Do you think her male colleagues are bragging about never asking for a raise? Doubt it. I bet they advocate for themselves and get their rates.

I suspect my tennis pal may be confusing being assertive with being aggressive. Because I think a lot of folks, particularly twenty-somethings, are confused about this.

So, what does being assertive mean? It means asking for what you want, directly and clearly, and while acknowledging the other person's humanity.

ASSERTIVE VS. AGGRESSIVE

When I speak at universities, I always get a lot of questions about this, so let's address it further. I think of being aggressive as demanding what you want without regard to anyone else's wants or needs. And I think that is unacceptable. You don't want to be that person.

But I also think of aggressive as pursuing doggedly that which your heart desires. And I think of aggressive as acting fast when urgency is called for, as in aggressively defending yourself. This, I think, is important.

When I was in my twenties, I was a segment associate producer, along with two others, on a show. A colleague informed me that the other two were in the boss's office at that very moment TRYING TO GET ME FIRED. When s —it like that goes down, you must address it IMMEDIATELY.

You'll want to know how this story turned out. I went in to see the boss when they were done, and I simply said,

"Bossman (I mean, I used his NAME), I have a question for you. If our department gets downsized, what will the criteria be?" To which he responded, without looking up from his computer, "Productivity." "Thank you," I said and marched out. Because I knew I was the most productive of the three. I did not get fired. One of the two out to get me did.

So you see, that was a time to get right on a fire like that and put it out. My reaction was both assertive *and* aggressive. (Aggressive in its timeliness.)

More recently, I was directing episodes of a show, and a writer had emailed my Executive Producer saying I had failed to deliver certain story points in the field. Wow. This was totally untrue, and I could prove it. I IMMEDIATELY searched the footage and gathered the time codes of where I had addressed those story points—and I had done so IN SPADES. I worded my responding email to them both very carefully, not wanting to reveal my IRE; but I defended myself, and the writer who complained wound up with egg on his face. Hrumph.

S—it like this gonna happen. I suggest that's the time for you to act quickly and defend yourself. Is it aggressive? Not really. It's fast, and vociferous, maybe, but it would still be considered assertive. I didn't *bury* the writer. I like him, in fact. I just defended my work. Only the speed of response—putting out the fire—might be seen as aggressive.

True aggression is disregarding the other person. Being assertive is declaring, or stating, what you want while simultaneously being sensitive to the needs and wants of the other. You can do that, right?

If you don't like that word "assert," if it confuses you, try this one: declare. Is that a more palatable word? Declare what it is you want. Declare it and see what happens. (If "declare" is too much for you, how about "state." Has a nice, neutral ring to it, doesn't it? "State" what you want.

My friend Crystal, the fine artist/muralist I mentioned earlier, said "A lot of things feel like moon shots more than they really are." How right she is.

You'd be surprised how asking can pay off! I am reminded of two old friends of mine who were a very successful screenwriting duo. When they had achieved some acclaim, they were offered a project they really didn't want to do. Concerned about saving face among the parties involved (agents, managers, studio execs, and the like) the two of them decided they were just going to ask for an outrageous sum of money for the script so that the studio would refuse them, and they could move on to other projects that interested them more. Only—the studio said yes.

It happens sometimes.

Spotlight: Yoshy (Aka Leonidis)
Tattoo Artist

"'STOP WASTING YOUR TIME ON DRAWING,'" Leonidis says her parents would tell her growing up. "'It's so hard to earn an income.' And materials were expensive, classes were very expensive. My parents didn't think I could make it."

After high school she studied graphic design, but found she didn't like the amount of computer work being a graphic artist entailed. Her life changed when she met a man doing tattoos at a swap meet. "He said, 'Do you want to learn how to tattoo? It's really hard, you have to read lots of books.' I didn't want to do that either. He said, 'Can you draw?' I could. 'I can help you order all the equipment,' he said. I said, 'I'm down, how much?' It was $140. I didn't have it." Yoshy borrowed that $140 from a friend.

She practiced at home, on herself, and on any friend who was a willing guinea pig. After a few months her mom noticed how good she was getting, and how much she loved it. "My mom told me, 'Go back to that man at the swap meet and get a job. I don't want to see you in this house tomorrow.' That was the green light I needed."

The swap meet retailer gave her a job doing small tattoos. "I stayed one year, but he kept me doing little things; he wouldn't let me do bigger. Eventually, I thought, 'I am very thankful that you opened the door for me, but it's time to go.'"

She brought photos of her work to a studio where a friend was working. But finding the right team of artists for a studio is always a tricky thing. "It's difficult to staff a studio correctly. You need different artists with different skills." The owner had all his stations rented out at that moment, but said he'd call her back in a month. "The NEXT DAY he called back and said, 'Can you start tomorrow?' I said, 'I can start right now. I'm coming in now.'"

As Yoshy progressed in her career, she learned how to get along in the studio environment. "There are lots of egos in this business. Sometimes you are better than the studio owner or an artist who's been there a long time, and they don't like that. There are lots of personalities to navigate."

At the age of twenty-six, Yoshy felt a calling to move to Mexico and practice her art there. She found it tough to get a job. "I'd come in and they'd look at [photos of my work] and they'd size me up and down and say, 'Is this really your work?' They didn't believe me."

After a year of pounding the pavement with no success, "I was watching my money deplete. I thought going to Mexico had been a mistake. I sent all my machines and inks back to California, thinking, it's time to go back." Just then a studio called and said they would try her out for one week. "I felt a little bit offended, but I said, 'Okay, whatever you want to throw at me, bring it. But I've sent all my tools back. All I have is my hands."

That was enough. "They never officially said I was hired. Every week they just kept saying, 'Come back next week.' The first week they only let me do small tattoos. I did not like it. I said, 'I can do better.'"

Yoshy is a good example of repeatedly advocating for yourself to work at the top of your skill level. "I have to stand my ground. I have really strong energy and I think they feel it. I'm professional, very serious, respectful, and I set my boundaries with people. I like to protect my energy. I go on vibes. If their vibe doesn't match what they're saying or doing, I'm out."

Eventually, Yoshy opened her own studio. "There are slow days. On slow days I paint and I go for walks. I tell myself the Universe is good. The Universe is going to send me what I need. I'm a very spiritual person."

Yoshy is following the energy and excited for what's coming.

"My life is gonna make turns. Canada and Germany are in my future because I have connections there that say 'Come check out the tattoo scene here.' This studio is not gonna end, but I will go abroad. I'm following what I feel. I'm nervous, but I'm going for it."

Chapter Six

Persist—and Don't Take it Personally

THERE WAS a time when I worked for a TV show called *Unsolved Mysteries*. It was my job to find compelling stories for the show. It was a top-ten network show, with 40 million viewers a night, and because of its popularity, people would write in from all over the country suggesting we profile their story.

I knew exactly what made a good story for the show, and it was rare that in my daily pile of mail an A+ story would come across my desk.

And then one day, one did.

A woman in Wisconsin had sent me a magazine article about the death of her son. He was found in his car, succumbed to carbon monoxide poisoning. The coroner ruled it a suicide. Only it wasn't.

I called the mother. She was surprised to hear from me. She had submitted this story idea to the show three times previously and never gotten a response. "Well, it didn't come across *my* desk until now," I told her. "I would never have rejected this story. This is a perfect fit for our show."

My point is this: Just because you are coming up against a lot of rejection doesn't mean there is anything wrong with your idea. What would have happened if this mother hadn't persisted *four times* in trying to get her story on the air? She would have gotten nowhere. As it was, we aired the segment, exposing the unsolved crime to 40,000 viewers, and generated dozens of leads that law enforcement used in their investigation.

If you want this career badly enough, you're going to have to persist and take it on the chin when you get rejected. This will almost definitely happen to you at some point. It doesn't mean you won't succeed down the road.

Tattoo artist Yoshy had a thriving career in Los Angeles. But she felt a spiritual calling to return to Mexico, the land of her birth. This was not so simple for Yoshy, as "I grew up in LA, so Spanish was my second language." In addition to that, she found that her looks and her gender identity initially posed an obstacle. "People are somewhat close-minded in my country. Coming back after many years, I'm not the same girl they saw that left. It was the first time many people were dealing with a person like me, a lesbian who dresses like a boy. In LA, I never had that trouble."

She continues, "When I started, artists were mostly male. They wanted to call me Leo." She went a year without working. She persisted, however, even agreeing to changing her professional artist name in order to work in a particular studio.

Now she looks back on her seventeen-year career, proud for having stuck it out.

HANDLING REJECTION

So great. You ask for what you want. The person receiving this request has their own goals and needs and—surprise— these might, on occasion, conflict with YOURS. Can you receive a "no" without falling apart? Can you bounce back from a rejection? This is a skill I suggest you cultivate, because if you are confident that you won't absolutely fall to pieces if you don't get what you want, you're probably more likely to *keep* asking. Which you'll need to do, over and over, if you hope to have a creative career.

Because sometimes it's the right thing at the wrong time.

The first time I asked a boy to a dance he said no.

The first time I asked for a promotion, they said no.

People can and WILL say no. And you know what? Life goes on. Sometimes the person—or the job—IS the right thing. But it's not the right time.

That guy I asked to the dance? He was still entangled with someone when I first asked him. The next year, he took me to his formal. The first promotion I got turned down for? They told me "Maybe in a year." I got it three months later. Even on that very show, they initially passed me over when I first interviewed, because of my lack of experience. But six months later they called me back, and I got the job. And it turned out to be a major break for me.

Yours is not to know the timing. Leave that up to the universe. But I think you must put out into the universe WHAT you want. And you simply can't quit pursuing it.

Remember that Academy-Award-winning movie *The Help*, starring Octavia Spencer? The author of the book the movie was based on submitted her manuscript to SIXTY literary agents before landing one! What if she had quit after fifty-nine?

My friend Christy had her first novel published by a major publishing house after submitting it to EIGHTY agents.

Conversely, I know an Irish actor who *almost* landed a major, career-launching role in a blockbuster feature film. Almost. He auditioned. He screen-tested. He got called back. They flew him to LA. He met the producers. He met the director. And then he didn't get the role. Crushing, I'm sure. I feel for him. But here's the thing: He's made that his story. He tells it over and over. I hope he won't let this define him. Because he can't make it if he does.

Every one of us who works in any above-the-line (i.e., creative) capacity in Hollywood—actor, writer, director, producer—we all have *dozens* of stories like this. But we don't spend a lot of time telling them. We don't create a persona around our rejections. We lick our wounds and we move on. Because that is what it takes to succeed at a high level in this business, and, I imagine, in any creative, competitive field.

Speaking of performing at a high level: Can I just invoke the spirit of Beyoncé for one tiny little minute here?

I remember hearing that when she was very young, and going through a romantic break-up, her mom would let her mope about the house and cry and be sad and stay in her PJs, and whatever she needed to do—FOR THREE DAYS. She had a three-day limit on expressing the sadness. On the fourth day, she had to get dressed, get out of the house, and move on with her life. And, dear reader, SHE BECAME

BEYONCÉ! Get it? I don't know her, and I've never worked with her, but that story always stuck in my head. I wonder if that brilliant tactic on her mother's part, that training at an early age, has just a little something to do with Beyoncé's tremendous success, excelling at such a high level in a creative industry. She was taught at an early age that losses are going to happen, you're allowed to feel the pain, and then you've got to change your focus and get a move on. There are things to do.

First and foremost, you've gotta ask. Anyone who's made it anywhere has asked for what they want over and over and over. I've worked on more than fifty television productions as a field producer or field director. Doors open for me. You know why? Cuz I knock. Again and again and again. This is how you get a thirty-year career in Hollywood.

AFTER A REJECTION

You don't need to fear rejection. It's okay for someone to tell you no. And if you know that it's okay, you won't absolutely fall apart when it happens. So *what* if you get told no? Life will go on. You may need to look elsewhere for what you want.

When I was a producer on a particular hit show, despite the fact that I really loved working there, I also knew that I wanted to be a director someday. And, as the leadership at that company was rather paternalistic, I knew they'd never "let" me be a director there. So I had to leave if I wanted to grow professionally. And now I've been directing for twenty-five years.

I worked on another hit show, this time as a director, and they had me supervise one of their editors who really, really wanted to be a director. I knew that the higher-ups honestly didn't think he was good enough at directing to be a director on the show. They thought he was a FANTASTIC editor. So I told him, if directing is something you really want to do, you're going to have to leave here. Because they don't see you that way.

Sometimes I'll even ask for what I want when I believe I'm gonna get a "no," just so the person on the other end will know that I know my value. I've done this sometimes when negotiating my salary. I've asked for X, knowing that a particular company's reputation is to underpay, and maybe I've decided that I'll work for them anyway, for some particular purpose I have at the time; but I still want them to know that I know my value in the marketplace. In my last job at one such company, my boss literally *laughed in my face* when I asked for a raise after a year and a half, and after telling me what an asset I was. Yeah. Stuff like this happens. And it never feels great. But at least he knows I know the score.

You have a right to ask. And a person, or the universe, has a right to say no. Can you accept that? Really? Can you REALLY accept that? And know that somehow your life will still be okay?

Do you have enough faith and imagination to even suppose that your life might turn out BETTER? Could you see that as a possibility? Even as concerns your dream job that Joe Blow got instead?

Be assertive. Ask for what you want. Know that a yes or a no will happen. In either case, life will go on.

When I was in my twenties, and struggling with all those

times I had to find the courage to ask for promotions and raises and the like, I read a very helpful booked called *Feel the Fear and Do It Anyway*, by Susan Jeffers. You're gonna feel fear. But you can't afford to let it immobilize you. Not if you hope to have a creative career. You just have to walk through that pain. Hey, if Beyoncé can do it...

Chapter Seven

Making Connections

"I CAN'T IMAGINE TRYING to get started in this business without connections. It's impossible."

I was backstage with a fellow producer when he made that statement, and went on to tell me who his influential father was.

"I did," I responded.

And it's true. I got into one of the most competitive fields there is without any "connections" to start with. I made a concerted effort to *make* connections, starting when I was a teenager. And it worked. Wasn't always easy, and wasn't as quick as I'd maybe have liked, but *possible?* Well, yeah. And it is for you too.

But let's say you think it's somehow impossible for *you* to make connections, wherever you are. Which, I gotta tell ya, in this age of Anyone-Can-Start-A-YouTube-Channel, Podcast, IG account, be on LinkedIn, Facebook, TikTok, Twitter (I mean X!), and whatever platform they come up with next, is *really really* hard for me to swallow, being that we are THE MOST CONNECTED PEOPLE IN HISTORY.

I'll accept that you think you have no connections in the particular world you want to be in. And you need them. So how to go about getting them?

You have to put yourself in the right environment, for one.

I worked on *The Dr. Phil Show* off and on as a freelancer for ten years, whenever I needed to make a buck. In general, he's not someone I'd want to emulate, but this particular piece of advice landed with me, because it happens to be something I agree with. Phil would say, "Put yourself in a target-rich environment." He would dole out this advice mostly to lovelorn young women looking for a man. He would tell them to go where the men are. Maybe it's *not* yoga class. Maybe it's the bowling alley, or the driving range. The same tactic applies to working in whatever environment it is that you want to be in. Get yourself there and get yourself around people who do what you want to be doing.

I recall a story about a man who badly wanted to be a pilot. So he got a job working the counter at a cafe. AT AN AIRFIELD. See the genius of that? Who do you think he served all day? PILOTS. Who were doing what he wanted to do. And he would listen to them and talk with them and learn about how they became what he wanted to be. And then they helped him train as a pilot.

Can you apply this to your world somehow? Here are ways.

You can intern. You can volunteer. I have a friend who is a lawyer in New Orleans, but someday he wants to work at the New Orleans Jazz Museum. Funny thing, busy as he is with his big-shot career, he always finds the time to volunteer at the jazz museum. Who do you think they'll think of next time they need to hire a lawyer?

My friend Megumi moved here from Japan, didn't speak great English, and was having a hard time getting work as a music teacher. I suggested she volunteer at an organization I was volunteering at that had a youth orchestra. Now she's been a paid music teacher there for ten years.

You don't even have to leave your apartment to make connections. You can join groups on the INTERNET. For free! Facebook groups, Meetup groups, the options are endless. And then go meet people. *In person*. IRL. Look them in the eye. Shake a hand or two. Have a beer with them.

There're a thousand more ways to do this now than when I was young and struggling, so sorry, I just can't accept that you can't make connections.

I was hired for a speaking engagement at an international symposium in New Orleans by a man I sat next to on a ten-minute streetcar ride. Truth. Recently, I reconnected with a Tulane professor I met during that engagement, and through her booked *another* speaking engagement this year. I just did a speaking engagement at Cal Poly University, which I was invited to do because I'm friendly with a professor there because she's in my ex-pat social group. And on it goes.

You can make connections in person, online, and by contributing your time and talents in some way. It's best to get out of your comfort zone and contribute.

When I was a teenager living in San Francisco, not knowing where to begin making connections in the media world and not knowing anyone who worked in it, I volunteered one summer for a Communications Commission run by an individual who was a local media personality at the time. It didn't lead anywhere. Not every connection does. But as time goes on, you'll find yourself getting closer and closer to the world you want to be in.

My friend Crystal, the fine artist/muralist I mentioned earlier, has lived and worked in Hawaii and Los Angeles, two of the places in the US with the highest cost of living. She networks in person, weekly. By doing that, she learned of an arts organization that subsidizes her rent. "I literally would not even have my housing if I didn't make connections and network." Crystal will tell you she's an introvert with a few social challenges. And still she goes to events, volunteers to serve on boards, and attends art openings every week. "You have to constantly put yourself out there in very vulnerable ways. The process of being an artist is that you are *always* doggedly pursuing it."

HOW TO NETWORK

This is important. When you are starting out, if you are an outgoing, friendly sort, you may think that the way to circulate in a target-rich environment, such as a conference or a networking event, is to meet as many people as possible. This is not the way. As someone who has been waltzed around at these things and introduced to 100 people in a night, I can promise you, you most likely will not make an impression on anyone that way. The numbers are just too high. Instead, when you go to, let's say, an alumni mixer or something of that nature, aim to meet a handful of people whom you spend a decent amount of time with—enough time to break the ice, get to know each other a little, have a laugh, share a story or two, be a good listener, and be REMEMBERED by that half a dozen people. This will serve you way better in the long run. Promise.

More time with fewer people. Quality interactions over quantity.

I always have this quote of Georgia O'Keefe's in mind: "It takes time to look at a flower. Just like it takes time to have a friend." Real friends take time and attention and emotional investment. So do real connections.

Similarly if you volunteer somewhere, be strategic in how you allocate your time. Rather than working one big fundraising event once a year with 100 people, do something that constantly gets you in front of the same group of people, so they can get to know you and your valuable contribution.

My friend Bonnie did this really smartly. She researched what charitable organization would get her around the kind of people she wanted to be around, and then she volunteered for them, consistently, twice a year, for thirty years. She focused all her volunteer time and energy with that one group, and it paid off for her. She's the first one they give perks to when they arise. This is more useful than volunteering here and there willy-nilly for all different kinds of organizations. Find a rich field and plant your roots deep.

Does your school have any kind of a program that promotes networking? I bet it does. Even if you've been out a while. What about civic organizations in your town? Churches? Theaters that need ushers? Museums that need docents? Publishers that need interns? Art studios that need models? Recording studios that need assistants?

There are just a million and one ways to make connections, and I suggest you get really, really good at this.

"But I'm SHY," I can hear you say. Okay, you're shy. Used properly, that can be perceived as charming. What would happen if you went up to a person you admired professionally and said, "I'm really shy, I'll probably do this all wrong, but I was just compelled to talk to you because of X." I have to imagine that would completely disarm your target, unless he/she was a total jerk. "No, Jeannie, you don't understand, it would be hard for me to do BECAUSE I'm shy." Yeah, I get it. But you're going to have to do some hard things if you want to embark on this path. And—news flash—you're going to have to do them over and over and over. It gets easier. Promise. It does. It's like a muscle that gets stronger with reps when you lift weights.

Like many writers, travel writer Jill Robinson had to negotiate the duality of being "inherently not an outward person" and the necessity of forming professional relationships and networking. She learned to "fake it really well and adopt the persona or attitude I have to take on to talk to strangers and go to conferences."

My pal Roger Suen, a film composer, describes himself as "Not a people-person. It's not natural for us composers." But he recognized the importance of making connections, and when interning on the Sony soundstage, he would approach other composers he wanted to get to know. "Not the mega-stars, but people whose personality was similar to mine and people I would have dinner with, regardless of their career. That worked."

A college student want-to-be actor asked me for advice recently. I told him to go to the film school and sign up to volunteer on student films. There he would be getting to know future directors and producers. I did that. I also volunteered at my college radio station and at the newspaper. And here's a funny thing: I knew a guy who volunteered at our radio station FOR YEARS—who never actually even ATTENDED the university! He just wanted to get to know other rock 'n' rollers who worked at the station and eventually they gave him HIS OWN RADIO SHOW! I don't think everyone knew he didn't go to school there. He looked the part, he showed up and contributed his time and talents, and he was accepted in that world that he wanted to be in. I just love that kind of moxie.

I assume you know about internships. I did three. I was a contestant on a game show, got to know the casting department that way, and petitioned them to intern there the next semester. Then I did two more internships elsewhere my senior year in college, as I got closer to needing an actual job. And it was those internships that, years later, led to all my first paid jobs, back when I didn't "have any connections."

Not having connections is something you can remedy.

Will you do it? Consistently? Over time? Even if there's no immediate benefit?

I had an associate producer I liked very much who left the show we were doing together to go work on the *Oprah Winfrey Show*. That was kinda a big GET in those days. So she packed up her LA home in about three days and moved to Chicago. We said goodbye and off she went. And then I kept in touch. For two years. Every few months or so, I'd send her a little email, telling her about what I was up to and life in LA, nothing special. She never wrote back. Not once. I didn't take it personally. Didn't take offense. We weren't best friends or anything. But I just kept doing it, without fail. Figured if it bothered her, she could tell me to stop, and that would be all right.

And then one day, she wrote back. After TWO YEARS of unanswered emails. And her subject line was "Do you need a job?"

In fact I did.

Her timing was fortuitous because I had just submitted my resume to the HR Dept. at Harpo, where she worked, because I saw the job advertised on the Producer's Guild website. Well, timing is everything, and though I'd done my own work to get the job, it doesn't hurt to have a connection on the inside. I also really liked this person, and it made me happy to think of her doing well.

She volunteered to personally walk my resume in to her boss, and ultimately I got the job.

There's a popular meme right now "I can do hard things." I'd like to change this meme to "Can you do things that take a long time?" Of course you can. But will you?

"MAYBE I DON'T HAVE TO WORK HARD TO GET CONNECTIONS. MAYBE I'LL GET *DISCOVERED.*"

Really? You're going to hang your hat on that myth?

Kind of on the flip side of people who think they can't do it because they don't have any connections are the people who think they'll somehow "be discovered." Except for Lana Turner sitting on the soda shop stool, this has NEVER HAPPENED to anyone.

Well, okay, I know of one.

In all my years in Hollywood, I know of ONE PERSON this happened to.

Do you know the actress Keri Russell, from *The Americans* on Hulu? This story isn't about her. It's about my colleague, Eileen, who just happens to look like her. Actually, not even. She's taller, and has a different face. But at the time Keri was starring in a network TV show in the title role *Felicity*. Keri had really curly, really long, blonde hair. Of just a particular color. And so did Eileen. And Eileen, who was a freelance segment producer at the time, on whatever non-scripted show she could get work on, out there hustling like the rest of us, working non-union jobs for modest pay, just happened to be having lunch somewhere in Hollywood on a certain day, when someone came up to her and told her she would make a terrific stand-in for Felicity. And that WAS a union job, paying way more than a non-union segment producer makes. And it came with health insurance and a pension—also unheard of in the reality TV genre. She was literally hired on the spot and did that gig for the next two years, an eternity in TV freelance job time, amassing a nice nest egg and all the bennies.

But aside from Eileen, I don't know, have never met, or even heard of, in my vast social circle, in my two unions and with all my connections, nurtured over three decades, that is the ONLY time I've ever known *anyone* who was really "discovered."

Oh, you'll hear anecdotes crafted to make you believe this myth, that the TV host you're watching was just a "regular person" before all this fame and fortune befell them. Poppycock. The TV chef who was just working in the local market, handing out cheese samples, when someone just

GAVE HER A TV SHOW TO HOST. HA! DOESN'T
HAPPEN. Every time I hear a famous TV personality tell
this kind of story I think, *Well, she's not telling you about her
years of auditioning as an actor, getting head shots, working as
a background extra, and hiring her dietician, trainer, and
plastic surgeon—all before she just suddenly landed her own
TV show.* Trust me. IT DOESN'T HAPPEN. It just makes
a good *story*. But don't believe it. Because it will take you
away from all the hard work you need to do (that *they* did) to
get yourself where you want to be.

The same goes with having your brilliant novel plucked
from the slush pile at a publishing house; being spotted by a
choreographer while you are dancing at the laundromat,
waiting for your clothes to dry; or any other fantasy scenario
you might be imagining for yourself. Maybe this happened
once, to someone; but it's very, very, unlikely it will happen
to you.

So.

Don't think you're gonna get away easy by merely
putting yourself in the TRE—the Target Rich Environment
—and getting discovered. Nope. Doesn't work that way.
Gotta do the work.

Fortune favors those who help themselves.

Oprah Winfrey likes the phrase "Luck is preparation
meeting opportunity." Think about that. You have some
control over preparation. Does that mean you have some
control over your luck in these matters?

Speaking of Oprah, I had the unusual opportunity of
filming with her in her hometown in Kosciusko, Mississippi.
It's a sweet little Southern town, but she didn't exactly grow
up right in town. More like, out in the woods. I'll never forget

walking down a dirt path to her grandmother's former house. Many times she has spoken publicly about growing up in that little home, without running water. Now she has a palatial property in California, a house on Maui, and a penthouse in Chicago. I've shot all over these United States, and been to forty-eight of them, and met thousands of people in my line of work, and I am here to tell you: Never have I seen anyone else come so far from so little. I have never known anyone with fewer CONNECTIONS starting out than Ms. Oprah Winfrey. Chew on *that*.

I had a colleague, Michael, who was trying to break out of nonfiction TV. We planned to meet up for coffee. He had been an AP of mine on a show and was working hard to take his career to the next level, and the first time we were supposed to meet up for that coffee, he canceled on me. No problem, I get it, life gets in the way. We rescheduled for a couple of weeks later. He canceled on me again. Now, I wasn't that busy at the time, since I was looking for work, so I agreed to a third meeting time, and he showed up. And this is what he told me. "I'm really sorry. I was determined not to cancel on you this time because I canceled twice already." Okay. "What's up?" I asked him. "It's just that I'm trying really hard to advance my career and network a ton, so I triple-schedule every coffee, lunch, and dinner meeting I have, because I know at least two people will probably cancel on me, and I'm trying to meet with as many people as possible every day." Wow. Interesting approach. Never thought about doing it that way. But you know what? Michael built a multi-million-dollar company and sold it to the highest bidder. So. That's how he networked. His way may not resonate with you. Find the way that does.

My way, when I'm looking for work, is usually to schedule at least two lunches a week with someone who is working in my industry. Here's the beautiful thing: You don't even have to say you're looking for work. They'll know. They get it. And I always offer to go to where they are working. I don't make them drive. Why? Two reasons: I'm the one who requested the meet-up, *and* if I'm lucky enough to meet them at their office, time and again I have run into someone *else* I know at that office, and now I've reacquainted with two connections in one day. Two birds, one stone.

Many times when I've run into someone else I knew, it's resulted in being booked for work. One time I was lunching with a colleague across the street from the Paramount lot, and a writer I knew walked by. We caught up, and she said, "Hey, are you looking for a job?" See: I didn't even have to say it. "Because we're looking for someone like you." After lunch I went up into her office, met the boss, and was immediately hired to direct some field pieces on the show she was writing. (Thank you, Stephanie Wilder Taylor).

So there you go. You may not have connections NOW, if you are at the very beginning of your process, but put yourself in a Target Rich Environment and go make some. If my pal Michael can triple-book every meeting every day, if I can lunch twice a week, if Bonnie can volunteer some place for thirty years, surely there's something you can do this week to have more connections than you did last week.

Spotlight: Jill Robinson
Travel Writer

"I FOUND my creative career in my forties. Travel writing is my third career," Jill told me. And boy, is she knocking it out of the park. If you read travel articles at all, you've probably seen Jill's byline. I know I have, many, many times, in publications such as *National Geographic, Travel + Leisure, Condé Nast Traveler,* and so many more, not to mention it seemed like every time I read the travel section of the *San Francisco Chronicle.* She's prolific in that world. So I was surprised to hear that travel writing wasn't the career she initially set out to create for herself.

"I went to a performing arts high school; I was an oboist." But she followed her energy away from becoming an orchestral musician "once I realized what my opportunities were and were not." Jill did the math and realized that there are only two or three oboe players per orchestra, so she'd be basically waiting for someone to die or retire for a spot to open up. And if a spot *did* become available, it would require passing a tough audition and moving to wherever the job might take her. Jill lived in the San Francisco Bay Area and really wanted to stay there. She would often ask working musicians, "What's your side gig?" and discovered that most of the people she talked to were music teachers. "And I'm not a very patient teacher," so she followed the energy away from being a professional musician.

She got an MBA and eventually decided she really wanted to be a general manager of a symphony orchestra. But even on that path, she noticed that "often to move up, you had to move away. That was my perception in my twenties." So she chose to stay close to home and join the booming tech world that was starting to define the Bay Area, eventually working for a startup that was an online travel magazine. Working in editorial sparked her interest in writing professionally.

Following the energy once again, "I would take writing workshops and attend conferences that interested me." Like many writers, Jill had to confront the reality of being "inherently not an outward person" and the necessity of forming relationships and networking. "This stuff is not gonna drop in your lap. If you don't ask, you don't get. You have to hustle." She says she learned to "fake it really well and adopt the persona or attitude I have to take on to talk to strangers, and go to conferences, and learn, and figure out how to break into travel publications as a new writer."

In 2009, Jill got laid off from her tech job and decided that was the time to go freelance as a full-time travel journalist. She had a mortgage, and a young child, and a supportive husband who runs a small kayak rental business.

"It took me a good three years to feel like I was making a living at it." In fact, she was very strategic in how she went about getting travel writing assignments. Initially, she'd pitch herself to write smaller things. "I saw that the *San Francisco Chronicle* did gear reviews, so I'd do some of that. I'd focus and pitch 'weekends,' and learned what that editor wanted. After I got confident with things like that, I'd pitch myself for other, bigger articles." Introvert or not, pitching is just part of the process if your dream is to be a travel journalist.

To date, Jill has traveled worldwide, and her bylines are practically innumerable. "People at the *Chronicle* thought I was on staff," because she has had so many articles published there. She tracks her money on QuickBooks, does a quarterly assessment of where she is financially, and evaluates prospective jobs against her own metric of pain vs. gain. "I maintained a list of clients based on what they paid and if the jobs were easy or if it's great to work for a particular client. Pay isn't the only consideration."

After the pandemic, like a lot of us, Jill re-evaluated her work situation. Prior to the pandemic, she was traveling twice a month. "I didn't have time to pitch the bigger stuff because I was always doing the stuff that keeps me in people's mind." Choosing to let go of some of the frequency with which she was published, in favor of working on the project that fulfilled her emotionally, "was a bit of an ego struggle, because people would tell me 'You're one of the most prolific writers I know.'" But she also felt the need to "spend more time pitching stories I care about." Now she limits her travel to once a month, noting "I still get FOMO. And Imposter Syndrome." See? Some things never go away.

If your aspiration is to be a travel journalist, Jill counsels, "You can't rely on pitching and writing. Be open to a variety of types of work. Have some stable clients as a foundation.

Maybe you have corporate clients. For example, I have a real estate development company as a client. They make big new communities with lots of houses. I do a lot of interviews of the people involved and write content for their website and their PR materials." This provides her with reliable, steady income—like a base salary, which she augments with the travel assignments she picks up each month.

Jill's a great example of someone who followed the energy as a mid-career professional and pivoted to rewarding, creative work that sustains her and supports her family.

Chapter Eight

Finding a Mentor

A MENTOR IS VALUABLE. If you can find one, consider yourself blessed. I've had three people I consider to have been mentors. I feel particularly bad for you if you're a twenty-something who worked remotely during Covid, and are still working remotely, because you haven't had enough PHYSICAL PROXIMITY to older, more seasoned professionals who you can learn from. It's a problem.

My first mentor taught me how to write for TV. My second two, concurrently, taught me how to produce recreations. They were incredibly valuable to me, and I'll be grateful to them forever. BUT: It's not a one-way street. I first had to provide some value to THEM.

I met my first mentor as an intern at *Entertainment Tonight*. He was a director there, and every Tuesday and Thursday, for eight hours a day, I transcribed all his interviews. For months. That's extremely tedious, painstaking work. And I did it for free.

At the end of the semester, when I was graduating

college, he invited me out on a shoot one day. It was exciting to be on set and to follow him all over the Hollywood Hills in his gold BMW convertible as we went from mansion to mansion, interviewing various celebrities in their homes and going to the set of a hit network sit-com to interview a major television star I had watched since childhood. (Turned out the star was coked up and kind of a jerk to the director, but that too was a learning experience.)

Eventually, this director hired me for my first real, paying TV gig, as a writer for a new show. He needed to delegate a ton of writing work to me (the entire show, other than the host wraps) because he was launching the show while still doing his very demanding, full-time job at ET. He needed someone to write well and fast, and so he trained me to do it. And I learned. Quickly. Trial by fire.

The second two mentors I had were when I was an associate producer (AP) on a show and wanted to become a field producer there.

Allow me a short digression on the work of a producer. Thanks to the movies, most people have a basic understanding of what a director does. Fewer people know what a producer does, in part because there are *so many different types* of producers. Some are in charge of funding the project. Some are in charge of guiding a story to its final form on film: hiring and overseeing the director, the writers, other producers, and all the department heads. Some are in charge of selling the project and/or getting distribution. Others are in charge of the budget, the shooting schedule, the day-to-day nitty-gritty of what it takes to get a production "in the can" (an old-timey reference from when we shot exclusively on reels of film that went into a film canister.) Still others oversee editing and post-production.

I've been both the nitty-gritty, boots-on-the-ground type of producer (generally called a field producer) and the shepherding-the-project creatively overall type of producer, the supervising producer.

I've never funded nor pitched nor sold my own project. I know my lane. I'm more of an artist, less of a salesperson. A gun for hire—although I've certainly had to sell myself to get the jobs. And as a director, I've definitely had to sell people (the crew, executives, the host, a cast) on my vision.

But back to the story of my mentors in the early days. On the show in question I regularly served as an associate producer for about eight field producers. That means I assisted them in innumerable ways. I thought about which of them were smart and kind and excellent at the job and picked the two I wanted to learn from the most. I regularly watched the show at home at night when it aired, made notes on the parts that were the most challenging to produce, and would go in the next day and ask these Field Producers how they pulled it off.

They probably liked this, because they knew I was paying attention to their work and was acknowledging the more difficult aspects of their jobs. It wasn't unctuous; I was sincere. But also, I was their AP. And you can be damn sure I contributed everything I could in that role to make their shoot days easy for them. (To be clear, I did this for all the producers I worked under.) I was fast and efficient and thorough. And they knew they could call me any time day or night to offer any help I could.

My point here is this: What are you giving? How are you

contributing? If you want someone to volunteer their time and energy as a mentor, what are you bringing to the party?

Because I gotta tell ya: When I hear an adult who I barely know saying "I'm looking for a mentor," without offering anything in return, or having any real prior relationship built, what I hear is "I'm looking to use you for your connections." *Hrumph.*

What you want to do is provide something of value upfront to this person, which, in most cases, is your time and your labor, and often for free. Then, and only then, do you wind up with the possibility of a meaningful mentor/mentee relationship. This is a two-way street. Don't be a succubus. These are relationships to be cultivated. Don't assume someone will just appreciate you without you putting out any effort. Consider what *you* can offer.

IN SCHOOL

My pal Kim, the fine artist in Arizona, mentioned earlier, who owned her own graphic design business, told me that while she was at the University of Iowa and trying to figure out her career path, as "there was no playbook," she wished she had cultivated a relationship with a professor who could take her under his or her wing and help her learn how to get support for her work. "As an artist, we have to apply for grants." (She advises all young fine artists to learn how to apply for grants, even if you just take an online course about it.)

You might be intimidated to reach out to a professor. I know I was! They were authority figures, and I was a teenager. I felt like the less one-on-one time I spent with them the better! But confronting that fear did benefit me, and Kim's advice strikes me as wise.

ON INTERNSHIPS

Do them. I did three. I found them myself—just called up television shows that I wanted to work on.

As an intern, I did all the scut work—proofreading and double-checking spelling of chyrons, clipping newspaper articles, filing, and lots and lots of photocopying. And eventually, it did pay off for me. But Kim makes a good point when she says "Make sure you're not just doing the drudgery. Ask them to put you in situations where you are learning what you really need to learn." That's great advice. I think when I was in my twenties, I was too ignorant, frankly, to ask for that. And that advice would have served me well. So I hope you do it.

When you are in your twenties, you have so much energy, mental and physical, that it's a great time to fit in internships with whatever else you are doing—school and work. As Kim put it, "Take full advantage of your full tank." My senior year of college I made a point to take lots of night classes, so that on Tuesdays and Thursdays I could intern full time at *Entertainment Tonight* on the Paramount studio lot in Hollywood. I'd drive to Hollywood for an hour, work an eight-hour day (for free), drive another hour back to campus, eat a quick dinner, and then sit in a three-hour night class. It was a long day, but that's not so difficult when you are young.

A lot of my early success can be traced back to that internship. It's a not a direct line—I never got hired at ET or the other show where I interned my junior year. But I met someone on ET who years later gave me an introduction to someone else, who brought my resume to a third person, who interviewed me, and a year after the interview, hired me. So, a long process to be sure, but it did pay off, eventually. Plant the seeds now. And nurture them. Over time. As much time as it takes. As you sow so shall you reap.

Chapter Nine

Mastering the Mental Game

IN THIRTY YEARS of working in television and interviewing luminaries from every field, it was a Canadian Olympian in sequins and Spandex who taught me the importance of mastering the mental game.

I was a producer on a network TV show meant to expose the seamy underbelly of the figure-skating world. The show was called *On Thin Ice,* and the title was the only good thing about it. After researching story ideas for a few weeks, we quickly realized that there *was* no seamy underbelly to the figure-skating world. This wasn't the NBA or MLB. These kids were squeaky clean. It was obvious that the show had been sold on its title alone (and perhaps some left-over intrigue with the whole sordid Tonya Harding/Nancy Kerrigan knee-bashing incident), and now we were in deep doo doo trying to come up with content.

Even if the show's premise itself skated on thin ice, it did give me the opportunity to interview and get inside the heads of some world-class competitors. They were an impressive group. Think what you will about the toughness of an athlete sporting a sequined toy soldier costume—I am here to tell you they are some of the most mentally tough individuals I have ever met.

Think about it: an Olympic figure skater trains for four YEARS for four MINUTES on the ice. That's it. In four minutes, everything he or she has sweated and sacrificed for, for YEARS (and really, a lifetime), is on the line. This is not a team sport.

When I asked Silver Medalist Elvis Stojko how he managed to land quadruple axles in the 1995 Olympics with an injured ankle, he told me, "I trained for four years of my life for those four minutes. All I can tell you is that if I'd somehow cut off my arm in a hideous tractor accident that day, I would have skated that night with one arm." Now THAT'S tough.

Elvis's story was visceral, but it was Gold Medalist Michael Weiss who really spelled it out for me: "By the time you get to our level, each of us has a body that is developed to its full potential. We're all equal physically. *It's the one who wins the mental game that takes home the gold.*" I never forgot that.

There's a special tenacity and fierceness to anyone who gets really far in a competitive world, be it sports or entertainment or medicine. It takes mastering the mental game to stay *in* the game. Keeping your head together, especially during periods of prolonged unemployment is key. I'm sure you've heard the cliché that there seems to be a link between artistic creativity and mental instability. I don't know why;

I'm no shrink, and that's someone else's book. But let's just acknowledge that people who feel things deeply enough to create art are probably going to feel pain a little deeper than most too. Or more frequently. It just seems to be the case. You'll need to combat this.

THE TYRANNY OF THE KITCHEN TABLE

When I was first out of school and trying to get a job in Hollywood (which, by the way, was what I did for the better part of two years), I'd get out of bed every morning with dread. I didn't know *what* to do. But I had all that discipline left over from all that studying in college, and I marshaled it to sit down at the kitchen table every morning, notebook, pen, and phone in hand, and try to come up with ideas of who to call to get a job interview. It *sucked*. Every minute of it was miserable. I didn't know who to call, or what else to do, and I didn't have a lot of confidence either. If I *did* come up with an idea for someone to call, I'd sit there for at least twenty minutes obsessing over and rehearsing what I needed to say. At this rate, I'd really only make three calls an hour. This wasn't going well. And the more I forced myself through it, the worse I felt, which was not useful when I actually got through to someone and had to present myself in a favorable light. Trust me on this one: No one wants to hire a depressed person to come work for them. It would have been helpful then to know the things I know now. The things I am about to tell *you*, so you can get through this part! Like how *not* to get depressed in this situation. Like how to combat the Tyranny of the Kitchen Table.

GET SOME SCHEDULE INTO YOUR LIFE

Something. *Anything.* Especially if you've gone from having a full-time job to having nothing more pressing to do than the laundry. Having some semblance of a schedule can really be helpful in keeping your head above water. Think about it: You've gone from having probably 40-50 hours a week, maybe 60 considering commute time, planned out for you, to facing this wide-open abyss of nothing but free time. So I implore you to find something, *anything,* that will put some structure into your life.

If you have to face rejection every day, trying to get your calls put through and interviews scheduled, *but only until 3 pm* when you will go to yoga, you will breathe easier, and it's not because of the yoga. Having something to do becomes a major relief. And it will put you in a better mood when making those job calls. And that will show in your voice, which is a good thing, because people want to work around happy people.

You can do yoga Monday, Wednesday, and Friday, and Pilates or pickleball on Tuesday and Thursday. You can babysit your nephews Tuesday nights, and you can have a regular Sunday night poker game or book club. How you design your schedule is up to you, but you WILL be happier with one. Add your activities as categories on your Board.

One of the best ways I know to put some schedule into your life is to get a part-time job—nothing taxing or stressful, or that will in any way prevent you from pursuing your career goals. And nothing where you will get roped in to spending more hours of your life at it than is beneficial to you. The goal here is to benefit your job hunt by managing all that alone time, that's all. I've done this a few times and found it incredibly helpful.

The first time, I saw a notice on a bulletin board at the park advertising a job as a "Part-Time Tennis Coordinator" at a very exclusive country club. I didn't know tennis needed to be coordinated, nor how to do it, but this sounded rife with possibility! LOL! I put on my best tennis dress and marched into the club.

"Can I help you?" the manager asked.

"What does a part-time Tennis Coordinator do?" I queried.

"Well, what do you do?"

"I'm a Television Director but I haven't worked in a while and I just need to get out of the house."

"You're hired."

The manager was a former soap opera actor, so he was familiar with the struggle it could be to keep your head on straight during the periods between gigs. He was thrilled to have someone with a brain, a Producer being a good organizer by definition, who was willing to work for $11 an hour, and I was thrilled to have some place to go three days a week. It was a win-win. The fact that I got to play tennis at a beautiful club that I couldn't afford and date some of the tennis pros was a bonus. I held that job off and on for years, coming and going between my directing jobs.

I did this another time in my career. I love to travel and I love to read, so I walked into a travel bookstore and got a job. (There too, the owner's husband happened to be an on-camera TV doctor on The Today Show, so she was sensitive to the vagaries of the business and only too happy to hire me, even though she knew I wouldn't be there forever.)

For me, it's usually at the three-month mark (three months of being unemployed) that I get restless and seek this kind of distraction. Three months of my own company is about all I can handle. You'll find your own limit. And armed with this strategy, you can avoid shipping off to the funny farm just to get a little company.

But let me be clear: Be sure to choose a job that does not use up all your mental, emotional, and physical energy and tears you away from your true creative pursuit. That would be a mistake. You need time and energy to create your art and pursue it in such a way that will lead you to be able to support yourself doing whatever it is you love.

I am reminded of an interview I heard on the *Freako-nomics* podcast of the playwright David Adjmi. At one point in his career he was "locked in a job as a paralegal in 30 Rock, and I was working all day and night and I had no time to write. And I was like 'I'm never going to be able to be a writer.'" What if he hadn't quit that job? The world may have never gotten to see one of the most Tony-nominated Broadway shows in history, *Stereophonic*. (If you're not familiar with it, it's about a rock band, and it's the show that rock stars go to see on their nights off.)

LOOKING FOR A JOB IS NOT A FULL TIME JOB

Oh my God, no. That will just make you a crazy person. And think about this: When you DO have a job, an office job, let's say, and you are there eight hours a day, you are not WORKING eight hours a day. You're just not. That would be rude. You must chat with that co-worker who stopped by your desk. You spend time getting coffee, reading the first aid poster on the bulletin board in the kitchen. You sign up to sponsor Harry for his marathon and buy those Girl Scout cookies. And then you spend time gathered around eating the Trefoils and politely inquiring about your colleagues' efforts to get their kids into pre-school. And don't even get me started on email and IG.

My point is that even having a job doesn't require constant, unrelenting *work* on your part. So why torture yourself with this fake rule that you must be chained to your computer and your phone in order to successfully look for work? Poppycock. Treat job-searching like a "real" job if you must. Spend a few hours surfing the web, make some calls, send out some resumes, and do some networking. Great. Go at a pace that feels right to you. But if it starts making you anxious or frustrated, if you start feeling hopeless and desperate, it's time to switch gears and walk away. You'll come back when you are in a better frame of mind.

I liken this method of looking for a job to my friend Mike's work method. Mike is a blockbuster screenwriter. He and his writing partner generally work for five or six hours a day, and that includes their outside meetings. I remember telling him about an aspiring screenwriter I met. This man told me that he was *so* disciplined and hard-working (did I detect a little bit of martyrdom there?) that he holed up in his Santa Monica apartment writing for eight hours a day.

"Well, he's not writing anything *good*, I can tell you that,"

Mike said. In his opinion, one simply cannot write at a highly functional level for eight hours a day. And I guess he knows what he's talking about, as he's been a successful screenwriter for twenty-two years.

Recent research suggests that four hours straight is about the maximum that anyone can really work at a high level creatively.

Another friend, Christopher, a producer who sold his own hit show, handles it this way: He job-hunts for a couple of hours each day, and then he works on his 1920s Victorian bungalow. Working on the house feeds his creative impulses and gives him a sense of accomplishment, which he carries with him into job interviews.

Yes, looking for a job is something you must do. And it's not all that fun. But it shouldn't take over your life.

LEARN SOMETHING

This is a sister strategy to "Get some schedule into your life." Taking a class will give you somewhere to go on a regular basis, but it has a lot of added benefits for the temporarily unemployed. Make this a category on your Board too.

One of the side-effects of not working is a lack of validation and sense of accomplishment. No one compliments you on how well you do the grocery shopping. If you can develop a new skill, you'll feel better. Over the years I've taken lots of classes, everything from improv to gourmet cooking. It's a great way to get you out of your own head and focused on something other than your job search or your lack of work. You'll meet new people and make possible connections. It increases your confidence when you have other things you are good at. And it sure helps with the identity crisis you can feel when you aren't working. I'm a television director, yes, but I'm also a trophy-holding tennis player and a pretty good swing dancer.

When he's not working, my buddy Roger, the composer, uses Google calendars to schedule out his job-hunting, "which is basically me spamming people" for one hour a day, and then he schedules four hours a day for what he calls "continuing education," i.e., studying music, reading books, and practicing. But he knows it's important to exercise (in his case, he's a badass rock-climber who regularly free-climbs Half Dome, using ropes) and makes time to see friends because he believes in "making yourself happy." He's smart enough to prioritize his mental health.

SOCIALIZING

For God's sake, get together with friends—another important category for your Board. I try to see one friend a day when I'm not working. Don't underestimate the value of this. This is key to remaining emotionally balanced during times of stress and to combating the isolation that comes with not having regular work.

One thing about having a job: It can provide you with a sense of community and camaraderie. You'll likely miss that if you go from staff to freelance or get laid off. Work on maintaining social connections, just for the joy of it. It'll really improve your outlook.

Plus, as you know, no goals are achieved in a vacuum. Sooner or later you're going to need others to help you. You never know who's going to be that person who makes that call for you and builds that bridge you need to get to the next level. Better to have those relationships in place now.

In my case, I've realized that all the best jobs I've had came when someone I knew thought of me, rather than when I pursued something I'd heard about. It's just the way it works. When I figured this out, I changed my job-hunting approach. Now, my primary form of job-hunting is lunching. (And who doesn't like lunch?) Tennis and hiking work too. I really try to keep up those relationships so that I will be present in people's minds. As mentioned but worth repeating: sometimes I've even gotten jobs *during* lunch. More than once I have been dining with a friend and run into another friend who has connected me with a job. If I had been home eating a tuna fish sandwich in my apartment that day, it would have cost me thousands of dollars.

Which brings up another point: Network with those who are *working*. I know it can be demoralizing when THEY have a good job and you DON'T, but your time is much better spent talking with people who are working (who —you never know—might be in a position to hire you next week), rather than commiserating solely with your fellow unemployed. Don't invest a lot of time in those nebulous "networking organizations," though. These groups can be places of "the blind leading the blind," where everyone is trying to get somewhere but has never actually been anywhere and sure isn't there now. Spend your time mining more fertile fields.

PERSPECTIVE

Get some. It's all around you. I know you want a better life-style for yourself. I know you want freedom from the stress of thinking, *I don't know what I'm doing. Am I doing the right things? The right way? Enough?* It's endless.

We tend to look forward at how far we are from where we want to be. But it's also worthwhile to look at how far you've come. Look back—I'll bet you've made a ton of progress from where you were a year ago, or a month ago. I know that if you've been using the The Board, you have progressed. You can take strength from these accomplishments.

Perspective is a beautiful thing. I was treated to a big dose of this one afternoon years ago in Rite Aid. I was having a bad day. Things just weren't going my way. As I headed to the pain reliever aisle, I overheard a woman at the pharmacy counter. I only heard three words, but sometimes that's enough. She said "My chemo doctor..." That snapped me right out of my agitation and back to reality. No matter how crummy things were for me at that moment, I wasn't saying "my chemo doctor." The size of whatever was bothering me shrank about a thousand-fold right then. See, I can't even remember what it was I had gotten my panties in a bunch about. Whatever it was paled in comparison to having a chemo doctor. So look around you. Or listen. Perspective is everywhere.

YOUR PHYSICAL HEALTH AFFECTS YOUR MENTAL HEALTH

You know it, I know it, so I'm not going to spend a lot of time on it. Feeling good physically has an impact on how you feel mentally. It just does. When have you NOT felt better walking out of the gym than you did walking in? I'm also a big fan of fresh air and sunshine (vitamin D from the sun alleviates depression) and lifting weights. (I've found that lifting weights increases my testosterone level, which increases my self-confidence.) You know what to do. Sleep. Eat well, exercise, and above all, be kind to yourself.

Chapter Ten

Get In the Habit of Saying Yes

OR AS MY friend Julia puts it, "Don't be too picky."

Julia was a self-described theater snob when she studied acting at Syracuse University. Her singular goal was to be a stage actress. Broadway here I come! So when she was offered a job at a television station shortly after graduating (a pretty good offer, in my book! I would have killed for that opportunity!) she turned it down because it wasn't the Theee-ah-tuh!

Now, as a director of career services for a prestigious art school, she knows better. "Don't be too picky," she cautions. Or as one of my early mentors put it, "When you're young, you have a lot to learn and not much to contribute."

I've made this mistake.

When I was just out of college and networking to get that first job in my field, one of the connections I made led me to a friend of hers who was working on a hit network show that needed a researcher. *Ugh*, I thought. *That doesn't sound like any fun at all.* After four years of researching term papers and the like, being a *researcher* didn't sound *Holly-wood* enough for me.

What I didn't understand at the time was that that role was actually a producer's role; they just gave it a job title that didn't match the work. The job was finding and pitching stories for the show, figuring out who were the best characters to tell the stories, conducting interviews, producing location scouts, and writing up the stories. And a couple years later—when I was working on that very TV show, in fact—I advocated to get *promoted* to that job and did it, very happily, I might add, for the next year.

Turning my nose up at it initially because I heard "researcher" may have cost me two years of career development. It certainly cost me thousands of dollars in lost opportunity.

My ignorance exacted a price. And ignorance is rampant when you're young.

My buddy Roger, who thrives in the competitive world of film scoring, recalls car-pooling with a kid when he was in high school who liked to listen to film scores in the car. "I thought he was such a dork for it." Fast forward twenty years or so, and Roger became a film composer, which allows him the time and money to pursue his other passion, rock climbing. Talk about living the dream! But he realizes he could have learned a lot if he'd done the same thing as the dork instead of turning up his nose!

My point is: It's easy to judge, scoff, and say no too quickly. You might want to say more Yeses.

I was made aware of the power of saying "Yes" when I was filming a very successful influencer and performer in his personal studio in Hollywood. The television show I was directing really had nothing to do with the subject matter of his art, but he did the show anyway. We chatted in his costume loft between takes, and he told me, "I always say yes. If I can accommodate it in my calendar, I will say yes. You never know where things are going to lead." I saw his calendar hanging on a wall downstairs. This guy is invited to participate in productions and events all over the world and has millions of followers. It looks like saying yes is working for him.

My friend Doyle, a sculptor, says, "Make it a habit to say yes. The key is to not be afraid" when you're invited to contribute to something a little outside your wheelhouse. As you'll read in the next section, Doyle's career, which began by digging up a T-Rex in Montana, is a prime example of how far this open attitude can take you.

Spotlight: Doyle Trankina
Paleontologist/Sculptor

"SOMETIMES I SPEND my day crafting alien nipples."

My friend Doyle is an amazing fine artist and sculptor whose work is in museums in several cities. He's also been a paleontologist, sculpted prosthetics and monster costumes in the film industry (hence the alien nipples), and worked in the toy industry.

In college, Doyle knew he wanted to be a sculptor; specifically, a representational sculptor. But he found that his undergraduate program didn't teach him everything he needed to know for that. So he got a job as a paleontologist with the Natural History museum where he had interned. "My first job out of college was to dig up a T-Rex in Montana." The museum needed someone with Doyle's talents and skill set. "Your average scientist isn't good with his hands. I had a lot of manual dexterity and I was fast. I knew how to handle priceless objects. We would collect rocks with footprints on them. An expedition is an amazing thing."

I bet.

Doyle became a fossil preparer, working on digs in Montana, Utah, and New Mexico. He sought the job primarily because it put him in contact with the kind of artists he wanted to learn from. "They were exceptional artists and craftsmen. They all worked on *Jurassic Park* and the *Terminator* movies. I got the training that fueled every job I ever had. I've never worked in an office."

The paleontology work was "hard but meaningful. It was a great job to learn problem-solving. We would be out in 110-degree heat. You were in touch with your body and in touch with the elements and we were really LIVING." And it was important to him that he was working on artifacts that would be in museums for decades, maybe centuries, and contributed to the culture and society as a whole.

When that job ended, Doyle worked in the film industry. The hours were long and the atmosphere often chaotic, but he loved the creative freedom that came with sculpting monster prosthetics, for example. "You don't have to be (excruciatingly) accurate when you are sculpting something fictitious like that. It's way easier than a scientific model of a dinosaur, which had to be accurate within a fraction of a millimeter."

Doyle next worked in the toy industry, which he describes as "Brutal. There was an unequal weighting around the speed and standards required, and how ephemeral the product was. You know it's going to be in the landfill in a year and is contributing to a disposable culture, and I thought *This is not art.* I'm not opposed to this idea of [standards of] perfection to meet," but he didn't want to apply it to the toy industry. He preferred his work as a paleontologist. "I was doing illustration, sculpting, but it was in greater service. I was working on something that was going into that depository of the public domain. That's important to do."

When I met Doyle, he was doing fine art production for a renowned sculptor's studio. Until then, I never knew that famous artists don't work hands-on on every bit of art they create! I didn't realize that the bigger the artist, the more likely they are to work as a director at that level, and have someone like Doyle to craft their molds, assist in the studio, etc.

Doyle found he liked working in high-art production, particularly coming on the heels of working in the toy industry. "It gave me things to think about; what kind of artist I am." That experience made him want to deepen his education. Just like when he sought the paleontologist job to get the kind of sculptural training he wanted, he pursued finding an arts school with facilities where he could learn how to cast bronze and expand particular abilities.

This required a move to Georgia, where he found the facilities he craved, and where he gave 110 percent to his training. "These skills come at a cost. We were often working on three hours' sleep, and sometimes it meant sleeping in my car so I could be in the studio first thing in the morning."

(My goodness, there will be no less than three other friends I'll be citing in this book that have slept in their cars at some point to pursue their creative goals. I'm not recommending it, I'm just recording the sheer dedication of my fellow creatives.)

After graduating, Doyle was freelancing in the high-art world and teaching part-time at a renowned art school when he ran into someone he knew in a parking lot who wanted him to be a full-time professor at that institution. This position allows him to impart some of the wisdom he's gained as a working artist to younger creatives just staring out.

Doyle sees his varied jobs as a real asset. "Diversity in your employment career is a good thing because it allows you to be flexible and adapt and see more of the world. Any job is a free education [—even the ones you don't like as much]. The toy industry made me a strong and fast sculptor. So the more you work, even if it's in different industries, that's a good thing. You could be a fine artist, but you should work with that interior designer, etc., because it gives you more to wager with."

This is my philosophy as a working producer/director as well. I always thought of it as "cross-pollination." My skills include writing, producing, and directing. I initially developed and honed these skills on a documentary-style show with re-creations. But I made an effort to work on game shows that had field segments, or talk shows that did, or hidden-camera shows that had that element, and that investment paid off. I became qualified to work in many genres and I expanded my professional network.

Like me, Doyle distinguishes between talents and skills. As he puts it, "Pencil drawing is not necessarily art. It's a way to think and problem-solve." So he recommends investing in yourself, and, in fact, finds that in today's world, especially, there's simply no excuse not to. "You have time on your own to learn whatever you want. Get off your phone. Pick up a book. Anything you want to learn, you can, on YouTube, on podcasts. There're podcasts on how to make it as an artist."

Doyle has supported himself for twenty years as an artist

and says, "I never marketed or pushed." But he acknowl-
edges that for those starting out now, "Sitting alone and
suffering in your studio isn't realistic, not now. And if you
are, you should share it. Platform it. There's a great desire to
see that behind-the-scenes work."

The way Doyle conducts himself is no doubt linked to
the wealth of opportunities he's had. His advice? "Make sure
you are walking around like you are investable, reliable.
Think of yourself as a CEO. How would you want your
CEO to look on Monday morning? Would you want your
CEO to look like he'd been on a bender all weekend and just
rolled out of bed after three hours sleep? Be well-rested. Go
to the gym. Keep yourself physically and mentally healthy. I
don't believe in this idea of insanity and brilliance being so
closely aligned. There *are* no more Jackson Pollocks. Don't
believe the myths that are out there. I don't think someone
whose life is a complete mess is making great art."

Chapter Eleven

Gratitude

A COMMONALITY I've noticed when interviewing my fellow artists is that they spontaneously share stories of gratitude for what they've achieved and those who helped them along the way. It made me wonder if it's no coincidence that successful artists live in a space of gratitude.

My photographer friend, Tammy, expressed such sincere gratitude for the wedding photographer who hired her off of Craigslist and really gave her her start. "I had a crappy camera, and she would rent a good one for me for $125 each time I had a gig . . ." (You see? Tammy even remembers the exact cost, twenty years later. It was *that* significant to her) " . . . because she saw something in me. Her believing in me and investing in me made it possible for me to grow and discover my abilities."

Yoshy told me about her frustration working for the boss who wouldn't let her do the larger tattoos she knew she was capable of. Yet even while she described her frustration, she mentioned, sincerely and emotionally, "I'm grateful that he opened the door for me."

I guess we always remember those significant individuals in our lives who had faith in us and helped us on our way.

After having been a field producer for ten years on many shows, I was being considered as a first-time union field director on a television series. This meant the company would have to sponsor me for membership in the Directors Guild of America, something that was going to cost them thousands of dollars (and, incidentally, make me one of fewer than three percent of the DGA members who were female). They called a former Executive Producer of mine and said, "We're thinking of making her a director, what do you think?" And he answered, "I'd give her any job she wants. She's that good." It's possible that phone call changed my life. That job vaulted me to a new level. I've made my living as a director (first single-camera, then multi-camera, then hidden camera) for the next twenty-five years, because of that phone call. And I have prayed/sent good energy for the well-being of that producer and his family ever since.

Here's the thing: The power in feeling gratitude on a consistent basis comes from feeling it *before* you have the really big moments of getting the big job or whatever. It's an attitude you can cultivate, even in the simple times. My skateboarding neighbor Rahaf (see her profile later), thinks about it this way: "You're telling the Universe 'Thank you! I like this a lot! More of this, please!'"

For some reason, a singular moment I experienced with a relative stranger years ago has always stuck with me. I was chatting with a trainer at my gym about—I don't even recall what. But I'll never forget her attitude. She said, "Look, I have a nice place to sleep and a nice place to eat and a nice car to drive to get me there." My gym was located on the west side of LA, not far from Beverly Hills, where there's a lot of striving energy and fierce competition in every field, and an overall tendency to look *forward* to all the goals and dreams you've yet to achieve. So I just loved that this trainer, who clearly wasn't dining on caviar on the daily, stopped in the moment to be grateful for all the good things she had. You don't always see or hear that.

I did something a few years back that might be helpful to you in cultivating gratitude: I wrote a letter to my younger self. I don't know what compelled me to do this, maybe it was my birthday, but it was lots of fun and it raised my energy level to attract more good things, I'm sure of it. The letter to my twenty-year-old self included things like "You're gonna travel to countries you've never ever *heard* of" and "I know you don't even exercise now, but you're gonna become an athlete and excel at sports you'll love—for decades!"

So.

Every once in a while—and The Board is super-helpful with this, because you've got those cards, that visual reminder—take a breath from striving, and *feel* the gratitude for how far you've come.

Part Three

Show Me The Money!

Chapter Twelve

Money MATTERS

MAYBE YOU ARE DELIBERATELY CHOOSING a freelance lifestyle and have full confidence in your ability to pull it off. Or maybe a freelance lifestyle chose *you* and now you are a little unsure about how to make it work financially. Or you're scared sh--less. Either way, I'm not gonna tell you money isn't important. It is.

Money is the key to freedom. Freedom to live the life you desire. Freedom to turn down the crappy jobs. Freedom to live more like a European and not work fifty-two weeks a year, if that's what you want. And it sure goes a long way toward being able to have work/life balance.

Getting your money right is the grease that makes all the gears work.

Personally, I've never been driven by the desire to be rich. Happy, yes. Rich? Nah. Studies have shown that if you are struggling financially, then yes, money makes a BIG difference in your happiness. It's important for your quality of life to have *enough*. But having more than that doesn't make an appreciable difference in your happiness.

So my goal here is to get you from 0 to 60 mph, as it were. Not from 60 mph to the Autobahn. These next few chapters are about getting you from a place of struggle to a place of peace, so that you can have a life *and work* that you love.

Chapter Thirteen

The Magic Notebook

By the time I was in my early thirties, I'd worked on a good number of television series. That's how it goes in TV. Long jobs are rare. I was staff for five years on an NBC show I loved working on, and then got made freelance. Consequently, my income was cut in half. Another time, I was one of three producer/director/writers on a WB show I loved. We were staff for the first year; then we all got made freelance. Again, my yearly income was decimated by tens of thousands of dollars.

Sometimes the funding for a show would dry up, and we'd all be laid off. On one show with a famous host I directed, we went from having bagels and cream cheese in the office every Friday to having to scrounge around on the floor, looking for pens and Post-its! And then the show got canceled for good. If you work in television, these things are a fairly regular occurrence.

The first few times these things happened, I would lie awake in bed at night, concerned about the loss of income and wondering if the money I had saved up to that point was enough to live on until I got my next job. It felt really insecure and scary. I knew how much money I had in the bank, but I honestly didn't have a very clear picture of how long it would sustain me. And I didn't know when my next job was coming. It would likely be weeks or months, but how many?

A reversal of fortune can be pretty common in a creative field.

And in case you haven't noticed, the gigs have only gotten shorter. Which means we are confronting this reality more and more frequently.

One sleepless night I asked myself, "Well, just how much *do* you need to live on your own in this city?" I know my *ego* was telling me, "You are thirty-three years old. You've been working in this business for over ten years. And with all your experience and skills, you *should* be making X." And I really *wanted* to make X annually, largely to feel good about myself. Plus I believe in people (artists, especially) being paid what they are worth.

"But, how much do you *need*?" I asked myself. "Because if what you *need* is a lot less than what you *think* you need, wouldn't that be great to know?" And yet a lot of us don't really know these figures. I didn't, back then. Knowledge is power, my friend, and wouldn't you rather KNOW that you can turn down a bad job offer, rather than assuming you have to take it solely for financial reasons?

I wanted a clear answer to that question: How much do you actually *need* to live at this level?

That's when I started tracking my spending in order to determine what figure I actually needed for my expenses on a monthly basis. I tracked it for three months and then extrapolated from that to really understand my yearly needs. Because even though I *wanted* to earn more money, for self-esteem reasons, what a comfort it was to really *know*, right there in black and white on the page, what I actually needed in order to maintain a good lifestyle. And you know what? Turns out it was way less than I thought it was. Despite living in one of the most expensive cities in America.

Knowing that figure was a game-changer. Once I knew it, I could sleep at night. And I didn't feel pressure to just take any job that came along. Because trust me, you'll get offered a lot of crummy jobs. And I would love to see you turn them down.

I came to think of the little notebook where I tracked my spending as The Magic Notebook. Because, like The Board, it's transformational. It can take you from feeling anxious and insecure to confident and in a position of power to turn down jobs when they don't suit you. And since the pandemic, especially, I think more people are realizing that they only want to take the jobs they really want to do.

I'm gonna say it again because it bears repeating:

Knowledge is power. And the effort it takes to track your spending is minimal. About ten seconds a day for ninety days. That's it. That's all. Will you not spend that amount of time for something that has the power to change your life for the better?

You brush your teeth twice a day for two minutes in order to have good oral health. Aren't ten seconds a day worth good financial (and mental/emotional) health?

THE PRACTICAL INFORMATION

Any small notebook will do. I like one that's about 3x5. Place it in your DROP ZONE. What's a drop zone? The drop zone is where you land when you come in your front door. When you first come home, where do you go? Where do you drop the mail, your keys, and your sunglasses? *That's* your drop zone. Keeping this notebook THERE is key to maintaining the habit we are going to create.

Each time you come in the door at the end of the day, you will pause BRIEFLY, and jot down how much you spent that day. You don't have to look at receipts; you'll remember. Truly. It will become second nature to you. Jot down the $20 you spent on takeout, the $5 to park at the mall, the $60 on the phone bill you paid, whatever. Jot it down. Close the book. Move on with your evening.

Yes, you can use an app, or do it on your phone, but having a physical space that you return to each evening is really helpful in *anchoring* this habit to a consistent place and a consistent time of day, increasing the odds that you'll succeed with this.

Because the key, like with The Board, is the CONSISTENCY with which you use it. It's the tiniest discipline, executed faithfully, over time, that yields the greatest results. It's the steady drip of the water that carves the stone. (You've heard the adage about saving $27.50 a day, right? If you can save $27.50 a day, that amounts to over $10,000 in one year.)

PULLING BACK THE CURTAINS: THE REVEAL

There's one more part to this. It'll take you a whole of maybe fifteen minutes, and only once a month. Personally, I enjoy it. Because numbers don't lie. They are clean and clear and simple. And they REVEAL things to you.

At the end of the month, using this little notebook, categorize how much you spend on groceries, eating out, entertainment, clothes, bills, etc. Reference your digital banking as well—any checks you have written or bills you have paid. Now total up those expenditures. Next, record how much money you took in this month. Not your gross, your net. How much of what you earned this month ended up in your hot little hand?

Now compare those two figures. They will reveal something to you. Are you living within your means? Are you behind? Are there things you feel could be cut from your regular spending? You'll notice them here. Are you in a position where you'd rather find a way to bring in more money, or cut some expenses? Maybe you want to do both. Are you in the great position of having money left over? Fantastic. What will you do with that money?

You might be tempted to blow it. You might tell yourself, "I can afford to spend way more than I am currently spending." And if you are at least midpoint in your career, then okay, maybe. But if you are in the first five to ten years of your career, I would beg you to save it. To build yourself a cushion. A nice, soft, comfy one, that will let you sleep at night. That will give you sooo much more comfort than 10,000 thread-count sheets, which, to be sure, I bought myself when I could afford to do so with no qualms about it. But if you are at the beginning of your career, you're vulnerable.

And clearly, taking care of yourself financially is a part of investing in yourself. For example, since I've known him, my sculptor/paleontologist friend Doyle has never gone for more than a month without work. Still, he's careful with his money. "I never go out to dinner. I never paid up for image. I drive an old truck. I don't buy the new iPhone. But I buy tools, and before I do, I always ask myself, 'Is this a tool or a toy?' How can I make my money back? If you want to buy a house, buy a house. But maybe buy one you can hold workshops out of." In other words, be sure your expenditures are *investments* in your goals.

Your first essential goal is to get from a position of insecurity to one of security that doesn't depend on anyone else. Not the "security" of a steady job. Because that depends on someone else. (Many someone else's, to be frank.) And that is no security at all. You want to get to a place of creating and sustaining your OWN security. So that when you are laid off or made redundant or downsized or fired or impacted by a global pandemic, you AREN'T so vulnerable. The storm is gonna come, so we want to shore up for it, prepare to ride it out with as few bruises as possible. Yes, the cataclysmic event, whatever it is, will toss you about like so much laundry in the dryer. And it'll hurt. But you don't have to get swallowed up by it. It doesn't have to be a CRISIS, neither financially nor emotionally.

When I was made freelance on my favorite job ever, after enjoying being staff for the first season, I was sad. I loved that job and I was disappointed that I wouldn't be doing it every day. But I wasn't *devastated* by the loss of income. I recognized that it was a financial hit, for sure. But I didn't have to take on the stress of being in a big hurry to find another job because I knew I had time on my side to find one. And I knew this because I had saved, yes, and also because I had tracked my spending. I knew how long I could go without working. And I knew it was four years. Now, I didn't know how long it would take me to find another great job that I loved, but I was pretty sure it wasn't going to take me four years.

That's the kind of power the Magic Notebook gives you.

Another time, I was offered a job working on a big-budget, prime-time network show. I hadn't worked in months and I was eager to. But when I learned more about the format of the show during the interview process, I realized that a core element of the show was deceptive: The unwitting on-camera participants would be deliberately embarrassed in front of a live studio audience in the final act. And I wanted no part of *that*. Even though I hadn't worked in five months, I knew I didn't have to take that unethical job. I was able to tell the executive, "I'd really love to work right now, but I couldn't sleep at night if I did this job." (He actually replied "I understand.") So I held out for something that suited me better. But see, I knew I was in a position of power to do that because I had a clear picture of my spending. And again, because I had saved.

Tammy, the wedding photographer profiled earlier, says that by tracking her spending and expenses, "Now I have a plan. I can decide how much I want to make this year, and decide if I need to book twenty-five weddings in order to do it, or raise my prices and shoot twenty weddings."

The Japanese have a system called Kakeibo that they've been using for—oh, just the last 100 years! It's credited to having been created by a female journalist. (I just bet she was a freelancer too!) It's basically a household financial ledger, updated weekly, that you start at the beginning of the month. It works similarly to the envelope budgeting system so popular on YouTube, TikTok, and the apps.

Basically, Kakeibo involves recording your projected monthly income and your anticipated expenses in four categories: Needs, Wants, Culture/Leisure (you'd put books, concert tickets, and classes in this category), and Extra/Unexpected expenses.

It's more time-consuming (weekly reviews) than my system, and perhaps not best suited for someone like me, who can't necessarily predict their monthly income, but I love it because it's a very holistic approach to financial well-being. It's highly organizational, and if you're one to "Marie Kondo" your closet, then you'll likely resonate with this approach. But what I love most about it is that (although Apple does have an app for it; of course they do) it really emphasizes *putting pen to paper* as fundamental to the process.

Research suggests that writing by hand trains your brain to process information in a more detailed and mindful way, and the meditative, intentional aspect of doing it by hand strikes me as both very Japanese and very impactful.

If the only way you'll track your spending is via an app, okay, fine. I acknowledge the utility of that.

Actress Heather Horton, profiled earlier, learned early on to track her spending. Now she uses an app called YNAB, an acronym for "You Need a Budget." Travel writer

Jill Robinson tracks her money on QuickBooks, does a quarterly assessment of where she is financially, and maintains a list of clients and what they paid in the past. Whichever method you choose, the important thing is to DO it.

A writer on the website MoneyUnder30 experimented with the process and found that she saved 35% of her income after one year. That's about par with my savings rate once I started utilizing my Magic Notebook. Either method is a deceptively simple process with profound implications. DO IT.

Chapter Fourteen

Watch the Pennies and the Dollars Take Care of Themselves

Using the Magic Notebook, you will see that most likely your biggest costs are housing, transportation, groceries, and health insurance, with eating out/entertainment probably in the mix. Let's explore each of them, with an eye to how you can save, so you can sustain yourself with less stress between gigs.

FOOD

Ya gotta eat. That's a given. If the pandemic proved anything, it's that Americans LOVE to eat out. For single people, especially, this can be a really important activity, as it's a time to connect with your friends and community. But eating out in this country is still fairly expensive, and doing it as a lifestyle will cost you. Even that burrito. I know this—because I've lived it.

Beginning in my twenties, I had a deep, burning passion to travel the world. I'd traveled around Europe when I was in college and I desperately wanted to go back. *Desperately.* So as soon as I got a steady job with a regular income (which took a couple of years), that was the first discretionary spending treat that I really, really wanted.

At the time, to go out to a quick lunch cost about $7. (I KNOW! Sounds good by today's standards, right?) So I calculated that if I *made* my lunch instead, after a year or so, I'd have enough money to go on a two-week European vacation. Not eating fast food at lunch literally saved me enough money to go on a two-week trip around the Greek Isles. And the memories I have from that trip, I've enjoyed for the next thirty years: I danced in discos watching the sun come up. Rode donkeys up a mountain top. Sunbathed on a beach called Super Paradise, lol! I'll never forget it as long as I live. You know what I have forgotten? All those burritos I didn't eat.

Funny enough, as I planned this vacation, I noticed some of my coworkers envying my upcoming trip. One of them, a producer I worked under, even said to me, "I wish *I* could afford a two-week European vacation." I chuckled to myself. I mean, who do you think made more money—me, an associate segment producer who booked *his* travel and ordered *his* catering, or him, a full-fledged field producer? (He made $850 a week more than I did.) I also happened to know that he had just purchased a living room full of Italian leather furniture for his apartment. And I also knew that it cost about the same as my trip.

Again, I'm not here to choose your values. If you would get more pleasure out of furniture that you can use daily and admire for years, then do that. But I have to say, it's been kinda proven that experiences lead to more happiness than material things. Any happiness study published in the past decade will tell you this. Just Google "the Hedonic Treadmill" if you don't know what I mean. (In essence, studies have proven that we adapt to the pleasure the fancy *things* we purchase give us. They don't provide as much pleasure over time as the *experiences* we have. For maximum happiness, it's better to spend your discretionary income on *experiences*, rather than *possessions*.) Millennials are really good at understanding this. Better than my generation. We Gen Xers came of age in the '80s of Gordon Gekko, "Greed is Good," and ostentatious symbols of wealth. Yuck.

Even now, I rarely go out to lunch for the sake of *convenience*. Meaning: I plan my days so that if I'm out and about running errands, let's say, it's going to be before or after lunch, so I can eat at home. If that's not possible, I plan ahead and pack a lunch and eat in a park somewhere for half an hour. That half an hour can save me twenty dollars. Five days of that and I have a hundred dollars. A year of that, and I have a foreign vacation.

Now, I'm not saying NEVER go out to lunch. It can be an important time for bonding with your colleagues, getting some distance from the office, or getting the 411 on the office politics, if that's your thing. I'm just saying, if you choose to do this, know its cost. *Conscious spending* is what I'm advocating.

When I began working in my professional career, my food budget was $25 a week. This meant I cooked without spices, which cost $3.50 a bottle. That was 1/8 of my food budget, and it just wasn't worth it. Decades later, my grocery costs are generally about $37 a week. And during lockdown, when I ate every single meal at home for a year, it was

$60/week. Twenty-one meals. $2.85 a meal. I eat meat, fish, chicken, pasta. Compare that to what you spend at any restaurant.

Not everyone wants to cook. I get it. There's a time cost, for sure: shopping, planning, cooking, and washing dishes. I understand. Several of my friends flat-out refuse to engage in this behavior. And they can afford not to. For me, it's a choice that makes sense.

Groceries are a substantial part of your budget. Want to know how to cut that by 20% every week? Read on.

Did you know that 20% of your grocery bill is due to *impulse buys*? Twenty percent! That's a lot. It's so high, in fact, that I wanted to test it by doing my own field study. So I did. And you know what? It tracks! I looked at my receipts when I got home and circled what I bought spontaneously that wasn't on my list—and I swear, even if it was just a few things, they always seemed to add up to 20% of my total cost! Crazy, right? But if you spend even a few grand on groceries each year, and you probably do, then cutting it by 20% is significant, no?

The other concept I've recently learned is to shop your pantry first. Meaning: Rather than going, *Hmmm, what am I in the mood to eat this week,* look in your pantry and fridge and freezer with an eye towards what's been there a while that you need to use up. Keep the old food cycling forward so you don't wind up throwing out things that have expired. Americans waste something like 30% of the food they buy. That's 30% of your grocery budget, yo. Think about it. If you're spending 3k on groceries a year, which I think is probably reasonable for a single person in a major city, you could save \$1,000. That's a plane ticket to a tropical island, for sure!

Also: The less often you go to the grocery store, the less you will spend overall. These companies are PROS at marketing, and you are no match for them. So stay out of supermarkets as much as possible. One good thing the pandemic taught a lot of us is that we can really stretch our grocery shopping to once every ten days, rather than once a week. Fewer times in the store overall means you're subjecting yourself to their advertising less, which means fewer impulse buys and fewer dollars that wind up going to Mr. Safeway or Mr. Aldie. That's a win, in my book.

And here's a radical thought: when you *do* eat out, you don't absolutely HAVE to drink. When I was in my twenties and really trying to save up a nest egg for myself, I generally would forgo a glass of wine with dinner, because that would add \$5 to my bill. (I KNOW! FIVE DOLLARS! Nothing compared to the \$15 cocktails I can afford to indulge in now!) I abstained so often that I overheard one of my regular dining partners say, "Oh, Jeannie doesn't drink." "Wait— what? Yes, I do." She thought I didn't drink because in all our frequent dinners out, she never saw me indulge.

I'm telling you—it's these little choices, made repeatedly, over time, that allowed me to build some financial security for myself. I'm not saying you shouldn't cut loose and have drinks with your friends. I'm just saying, when money is really, really tight, this might be a simple place to cut that's often overlooked and taken for granted.

HOUSING

This is a big, tough thing, I know. Particularly now. But even decades ago, when rents were more affordable, I've personally known three TV professionals—two gaffers (set electricians) and my friend Greg, a cameraman—who lived out of their cars when they were starting their careers. Not ideal, and I'm not recommending it, but it does give you some idea of the lengths people will go to while launching their creative careers. I have mad respect for them and their skill of delayed gratification. I will always and forever hire people with that level of devotion to their chosen field.

TRANSPORTATION

It's amazing to me that people take for granted that the only way to get anywhere is to fire up 4,000 pounds of steel anytime you need to run an errand.

If you don't know this, you should: A car depreciates by 20% the minute you drive it off the lot. Why should you be the one to bear that cost? I've never purchased a new car. There is an argument for doing so—provided you keep it a really long time. What works for me is to buy a car that is a little bit used—a few years old with 20,000 or so miles on it. The depreciation cost was paid by the first owner, not me. Lease returns are a good bet, but I've also bought from individuals and feel that you are more likely to find a decent, honest, random person than a decent, honest used car dealer —but hey, that's just me.

More radically: Ask yourself, Do you really, really NEED a car? I know you think you do. Those quintessentially American values of freedom and independence—we're all about the personal automobile. I live in Southern California—we INVENTED freeways. We are the ultimate car culture. But I ask you to question this, because you can save a lot of money in this category. A car costs me in gas, maintenance, insurance, car washes, registration, and parking. It costs me literally THOUSANDS of dollars a year. And that's *without* a car payment! I choose to have a car. But consider making another choice.

I know a lawyer in San Francisco who gets by without a car. She uses Zipcar when she needs one.

I know a married couple, both high-net-worth individuals working at Rand, who share one small car and walk to work. In case you're not familiar with the Rand Corporation, it's essentially a think tank where some of the most brilliant minds in this country have worked for decades, and most every employee has a PhD. What I'm saying is, they're smart, highly educated people. I like to model my behavior after people like that.

Car Pooling. I find that very few professionals do this. But I've done it twice in my career, when I was making a good living, producing on two different network TV shows. In each case, there was another solo colleague traveling from one part of LA to another, a good hour and a half of commute time each day, so why NOT carpool? It's good for the environment, it's good for socializing, and it's good for your personal bottom line.

HEALTH INSURANCE

For me, this has always been really important. I just believe in having it. In this country, sadly, a health crisis can bankrupt you. To my way of thinking, you need to protect against this. I don't care what kind you get, but get some.

Many—probably most—creative careers are comprised of a series of projects or gigs, none of which offer benefits. Maybe only for three or four years, cumulatively, did I *ever* work for an employer that offered health insurance. So you need to wrap your head around buying your own and just do it. Religiously. HUGE PRIORITY. Historically, it's always been one of my biggest costs, but I've managed it in every single year, even the year when I worked a total of twenty-seven days. Work it out. Make it happen.

ENTERTAINMENT/EATING OUT

There's so much opportunity for getting together with friends outside of bars and restaurants. Didn't the pandemic teach us this? A hike, a walk on the beach, riverfront, or downtown, a picnic, a museum on their free day—all of these can get you the socialization you need without shelling out a ton of bucks. I sometimes offer to meet colleagues while they are walking their dog instead of always meeting them for happy hour or lunch. We're getting our exercise, and it's a win-win. Hopefully you have a park close to you. Can you play basketball, softball, tennis there? You pay for these spaces with your taxes. Enjoy them.

AVOID ADVERTISING

One thing Americans are really, really good at is marketing. You can't sit quietly in a taxi in New York anymore or pump gas in LA without being marketed to by the loud video playing in your face. It's so pervasive. Do what you can to avoid advertising, cuz it sneaks in there and tickles your subconscious and causes dollars to take flight from your wallet. I have several friends who don't watch TV or YouTube. That's one way to avoid it. Staying out of malls and limiting time on the internet and the socials are another. I gave up most magazines long ago.

ON DELAYED GRATIFICATION

I'll never forget an article that I read in the *LA Times* in the nineties. Yep, it was that long ago, but I've never forgotten it for its poignant example of delayed gratification. A young couple from Vietnam moved to Los Angeles, to work in a bakery. For that first year, they slept in the back room of the bakery. That was their home. For a YEAR. No car, no TV, no "mod cons," (modern conveniences) just a back room of a bakery, where they worked every day. You've heard rags-to-riches stories like this before, I'm sure. Here's where it takes a twist.

After a year, the husband says to the wife, "We have enough money to move out now and get an apartment on our own." But if we do this for one more year, we will have enough money TO BUY OUR OWN BAKERY."

Now. Think about that. The story made such an impression on me because I couldn't IMAGINE any American couple making that choice. To forgo creature comforts like a bedroom or a bathroom FOR TWO YEARS in order to set themselves on a path for their future financial security. Mad Props. Much respect. Delayed gratification on steroids. If they can do this—can you maybe just bring your lunch to work? Just sayin'.

BEING FRUGAL VS. BEING CHEAP

I am not advocating being cheap. I am advocating frugality. What's the difference? Frugal is making choices to put your money where your values are.

You love your friends? You show up to their parties, you bring a gift to someone who is hosting you. You give to charity. Maybe you tithe. When it's a matter of choices, frugal people make choices that align with their values.

Cheap is putting the value of MONEY above other higher-vibration values. It's valuing money for money's sake. That's sad. If you can afford to use your money in a way that aligns with your values, a way that would benefit your quality of life, and you *don't* do it because you'd rather sit back and count your piles of gold, then I think that's miserly. You don't want to be that person. You want to be the person who can give to yourself and your friends and be generous and kind, easily and without regret.

I know what I said earlier about cars, and for many years now, I've driven nicer cars. Would I have a lot more money in my bank account if I didn't? Of course. But I live in a car-oriented city that lacks great public transportation and I've always had a pretty substantial commute to my jobs, and because I spend a fair amount of time in my car, sitting in the most intense traffic in America, I've decided that a nice car benefits my quality of life. If I lived in a small town, or a city with great public transportation, or certainly if I couldn't afford to pay for it outright with no car loan, I wouldn't buy such a car. It's a conscious choice. That's what I'm advocating: conscious spending as opposed to unconscious.

CREDIT CARDS

Without question, the mindset I'm advocating means you do not accrue interest on credit cards. Duh. You do not charge in excess of what you can pay off at the end of the month. Period, double stop. Do I even need to say this?

I like how Elizabeth Gilbert, author of *Eat, Pray, Love*, articulates it in her excellent book on creativity, *Big Magic*: Debt will always be the abattoir of creative dreams.

As long as you can have some fun, whatever that looks like for you, and make decisions that support your personal values, you won't regret living frugally. Promise.

There are so many creative ways to save money.

(For more on this, especially for the twenty-something readers, go to my website: Jeannie-ONeill.com)

Spotlight: Allan Kraut
Live Sound Engineer

ALLAN IS A LIVE SOUND ENGINEER—THE person you see working the mixing board at concerts—but he was going to be rock star.

"Music is all I ever wanted to do since high school." Allan attended the prestigious Berklee College of Music in Boston. He got in on a loophole. "If I attended the summer program at Berklee, then I wouldn't have to audition." Which was great for Allan, because although he was a good guitarist, he couldn't read music.

"I had what they would call ADHD today, but in the eighties they didn't really do that. I had an anger problem, and I would burn things and break things. I was in rock bands and played electric guitars, and that really helped."

At Berklee, he realized that he wasn't in the very top tier of musical ability. "I dropped out and got a degree in business and finance because I thought 'I'm not gonna be able to make a living in music.'" He then went on to make his living with music for the next twenty-five years.

"I fell into live sound engineering because I was doing lights at a club in Boston." The clubs in Boston were all using the same sound engineer at the time. "He was abrasive, and eventually they said 'You've got a good personality, and you can't teach that. We'll teach you how to do sound.' I was reliable and not on drugs and they taught me and I started working the events.

"You play your analogue mixing board like an instrument. You're like the other person in the band who isn't on stage. It satisfied my creative tendencies."

Allan was enjoying himself working at the clubs every night when "out of nowhere, someone came up to me and asked, 'Would you like to teach at a college?'" So he did, part-time. He would teach in the daytime and mix bands in the clubs at night.

After about a year of doing this, a friend of his who had been mixing for New Kids on the Block and the Backstreet Boys asked him if he wanted to take a job as the monitor engineer for NSYNC. They were about to embark on their European tour. This was the big leagues.

It was the start of the semester, and Allan had only taught one class session when he got this amazing offer. He went to his employers at the college and told them he would need to be replaced for the year because he was going on tour. His employers let him know that he would not be able to return to his teaching job if he left. He understood the consequences of touring meant burning that bridge.

Allan also knew that "If you say no [to a job] like that, they [the touring musicians] stop calling." He faced a crucible moment.

He thought deeply about the choices before him, and decided he really wanted the lifestyle that teaching audio engineering provided him. "I was in my late twenties and I wanted a relationship. I had known sound engineers who go on the road all the time. They were divorced and surly, had drug problems, and were living that all-night-party lifestyle. I *liked* teaching. I liked having a schedule and health insurance." So he followed the energy and turned down the band gig. Looking back, Allan says, "I'm glad I chose the path I did."

For the past twenty-five years, Allan taught dozens of aspiring rock stars at the music school. "My students, they didn't know what they wanted to do. They would all say 'I want to be a producer,' and what they mean is 'like Dr. Dre.' I told them that thousands of students like you have come through here and only one had a hit song. Those are bad odds. We'll show you how to do that, produce music, but we're also going to show you things that are practical. For instance, you can make a perfectly good living doing sound engineering for gigs like the dentists' convention." (I don't know why we all have this fixation with dentists! LOL!) "Audio is an applied art. Know the difference between fine and applied art."

Allan continued to work live gigs while teaching because he wanted to keep current on all the technology. He waxes poetic about the days of the analogue mixing boards. "With analogue, you felt like you were playing an instrument. Now it's like setting up 100 printers in an office. It's sooo unsexy. But I still kept working for Live Nation and others because I had to know the new equipment."

Allan found a good blend of professions that fed his creativity and allowed him to live a good quality of life. When I met him and his wife, Julia, they had just left their jobs to travel the world for a year. More on how they managed this financially in the next chapter.

Chapter Fifteen

Creating Security

I KNOW what's stopping a lot of you from pursuing your dreams: this idea of "security." "Of course I want to pursue my dreams, but what about *security?*"

My friends, there IS no such thing as "security" in the way that generations past would talk about it.

My father worked for the same company for thirty-seven years. Can you *imagine* that today? Probably not, because it no longer exists. You may have a steady, high-paying job you love—and still get canned unexpectedly. This happened recently to several of my friends who had highly sought-after positions in tech at movie studios. They *loved* their jobs. And excelled at them. It just didn't matter. Another friend, an attorney and VP of business affairs at a major studio, was just ousted as part of a 600-person layoff.

There are all kinds of reasons for being let go that you can't control. This is why you may as well do work you love and *create your own* internal security. Because external security is just an illusion. And if you're not buying into a false notion of security, it goes a long way toward being able to commit to choosing work you love.

I'd like you to rethink the notion of "security," so you don't let it stop you from pursuing your dreams.

What would it take for YOU to feel secure? *Specifically?* $100k in the bank? A million? A job where you'd never ever ever get fired? Being your own boss? What?

And how do you square that with a freelance career and an unsteady income? What about the very real possibility—or, in my experience, inevitability—of being fired, laid off, downsized, "made redundant," or a hundred other ways of being kicked out of the sandbox? That doesn't sound too secure, does it?

If you're going to thrive as an artist or a creator, the *work* might very well be unstable—which is why *you* can't afford to be. It's critical to set yourself up so that you can thrive *despite* the ups and downs of a creative career with an itinerant income.

Security means something different to everyone. No doubt you have your own definition, but try this one on for size:

Security is knowing how long you can support yourself on the money you've accumulated. Security is never having to take a job you don't want, strictly for financial reasons. If you have time on your side, then you don't have to trade the hours of your life for a job you don't want to do.

What do I mean by having time on your side? I mean amassing a couple of years' worth of your living expenses. That's it. Can we agree that it probably won't take you a couple of *years* to get another job?

The simplest, fastest way to do this is to live well below your means. Then you can more quickly amass an amount of savings and investments that you could draw on if the s—t hits the fan. Wouldn't you sleep better at night knowing you have that financial cushion? Would that knowledge in turn benefit your mental health by reducing your stress?

If saving this amount of money seems impossible from where you are right now, I get it. I've been there too.

It took me a couple of years to get my career off the ground. During that time I shared a bedroom—not just an apartment, but a bedroom, with two twin beds—in a lousy neighborhood, and drove a thirty-year-old car that broke down every three months and cost $300 to repair each time. And then my roommate moved out, leaving me to pay the entire cost of the apartment's rent, which I could not afford on my $10 an hour. salary as a television segment producer. (Yes, the same salary I could have made working at the mall.) My grocery budget was $25 a week for years. It was wasn't fun. But that's what it took to live in the city of my dreams, where I could manifest my career goals, given enough time and effort. And eventually I got a break. I got a steady TV job that paid $13 an hour. That wasn't a lot either, but I got promoted after five months, and little by little, my situation improved.

Now, years later, I'm sitting on the balcony of my country club, overlooking the pool, as I write this. I play tennis here regularly, even during the week, because I do not have to work fifty-two weeks a year. I use that downtime to travel for fun, internationally once or twice a year, and domestically about once a month. Travel is one of my greatest passions so I made sure to set up a lifestyle that would support that.

How on EARTH can I afford this lifestyle on a modest and very unstable income? By living small in order to live large.

I'd like to pause here and say I am the eternally grateful beneficiary of a four-year university education, which I did not have to fund myself (I paid 20% of it by working summers and winter holidays), which I acknowledge to be a *tremendous* benefit and privilege. I graduated with a mere $5,000 in debt—unheard of in today's climate. I also had all the benefits of growing up in a major American city and I hit the jackpot by being born to not just one, but two parents who cared about me and were paying attention. So yeah, I am the product of some privilege, to be sure. White, and otherwise.

Also true is that I've managed to support myself since the age of twenty-one in the most fickle of businesses. One does not come to Hollywood looking for job security. And very quickly I learned that in order to live out my dream in *the city* of my dreams, I was going to have to live small, at least in the beginning. (Or marry rich, I guess, but that wasn't my plan.)

I'm going to say it again because it's so important: The easiest path to your financial security is to live well below your means.

Keeping The Notebook will show you when you have months where you've made more than you need to just get by. SAVE it. And INVEST some of it. Early and often, and as much as you feel comfortable with. The one thing I always hear women, in particular, who are good savers and investors, say is "I wish I had started earlier." Why is it we don't do that? I don't know, and that's someone else's book, but I suspect it's fear. I know it was with me. After my first two struggle years (I made $4,000 my first year out of school and $7,000 the second year) I think I was always waiting for the other shoe to drop, and investing in a market that goes up and down (be it the stock market or the housing market) felt way too scary. But almost everyone who is financially secure says they wish they had started investing sooner.

Like a lot of us, Tammy, the wedding photographer profiled earlier, has struggled with this. "I wish I had educated myself on money and investing. I'm forty-six and just now getting my s—t together. I was always good at saving; I have a hoarder mentality. I wasn't good at investing. [That's common among people who are good savers.] Now there's so much info on social that's free!"

She's right, and some of it is quality information.

Perhaps you've heard of the FIRE Movement: Financial Independence Retire Early.

Now, I'm not necessarily advocating retiring early. I'm advocating having work that you LOVE, that is good for you. That allows you to contribute to society in a way that feels meaningful to you. We humans LOVE meaning, don't we? But I most certainly *am* advocating the FI part of FIRE, Financial Independence. Because that will set you free. (I'm okay with the E part of it too. Early is good, if that's what you want. Good for you. It's just the R that I'm ambivalent about. My gut says it's better to be engaged with work you love than to retire. To be engaged in creating.)

There's a lot to be learned from the FIRE Movement. You might look up Mr. Money Mustache, who lays out the income vs. savings formula pretty clearly; plus there are many books and YouTube channels on it that can help you with specifics regarding what kinds of numbers you need to be financially independent, which translates to the luxury of being choosey about the jobs you will take. Because you should *enjoy* the hours of your life. I'm not really down with the faction of the FIRE folks who choose extreme frugality to the point of penury. I'd rather see you in a position to enjoy a good quality of life, as soon as possible. So I guess I'm less FIRE and more FIQOL - Financial Independence/Quality of Life.

FIRE aside, most of us who have achieved longevity in any creative field have learned how to live small before living large.

Allan, the sound engineer, said he decided early on to live "like a college student," meaning with very low overhead. He contrasts his lifestyle with a friend of his who's a very successful film composer. "He has three houses now and kids in private school. The lifestyle just creeps up on you, and now you have this high overhead. But the thing is, those people aren't necessarily happier than you are."

Recently, Allan and his wife, Julia, invited me to join them on a twenty-one-day cruise from Europe to Southern Africa. They live in a nice apartment in a marina and enjoy a pretty great quality of life, if you ask me, because both believe in living small to live large. Julia says, "The whole point was to not be stressed out. It's so easy to fall into debt, but you need to get out ahead of that hamster wheel." Both of them are great at living below their means so that they can live the creative lifestyle they want.

David Adjmi, the hit Broadway playwright mentioned earlier, was scraping to get by early in his career when he received a $25,000 grant in 2003, a windfall. As recorded in a *Freakonomics* podcast, he thought, "Well, I can really make this last if I move to Germany." So he moved to Berlin, where his rent was $200 a month. He went on to say "That's how I generated the beginning of the body of work that made my name." Talk about thinking outside the box about how to live small!

My buddy Roger, the film composer with lots of credits to his name, including an Oscar-winning film on which he worked as a ghostwriter, says, "It's very unsexy, but basic personal finance is a must. I started doing it a couple years into my career. Some years, you can't have that emergency fund—I've bled it many times." But he lands on his feet, went out on his own after working for others, and now owns a house by the beach.

My colleague Jen came to Hollywood to reinvent herself in her thirties after working in marketing in NY. She rented a room for $400/month. After a year of temping, she got hired as a producer's assistant, then an associate producer, then a Producer, doubling her salary. She moved, bought a better car, did all the expected things. But she tells me now that she wishes she had continued living cheaply because, "No one cares where you live. No one cares what you drive." Having learned that lesson, she now lives in a self-described "crappy apartment," but you know what? She took *seven* vacations last year! Including renting a house in her favorite country for a total for a total of three months!

Crystal, the fine artist described earlier, has enjoyed working and living in Hawaii and Los Angeles, two of the most expensive places in America. Would you forgo a few purchases a month in exchange for living in one of those iconic places? Crystal does. "I make sure not to spend more than $100 a month on things that aren't necessary."

Leonidis aka Yoshy, the tattoo artist who moved to Mexico when she was twenty-six, found that she had days when she couldn't work due to illness. This never happened in LA. After experiencing this a few times, she realized she had to set aside some savings for herself to tide her over during the times she couldn't work. "In LA, I was helping my parents, but I always had money coming in. I never thought of opening a bank account. But I got sick a lot when I moved to Mexico because of the food I ate. I thought, 'I need to start a savings account now because of the slow times.'" She's also noticed that there are more tattoo artists working now than there were when she started in the business seventeen years ago, so competition for jobs is more fierce than it was previously. Consequently, "Now when there's a lot of work, I save as much as I can."

So remember: Even when things are good and the employment is plentiful, most of these creative jobs aren't terribly long-term, compared to the "normie" jobs out there. It seems pretty clear that the gig economy is more and more profligate and here to stay. You don't know what your next job will be or when it will come. And you can't control that. What you CAN control is what you do with the money you bring in.

It's up to you to create security for yourself.

If you're using the Magic Notebook, you're taking steps

to create your financial security. And by following the suggestions laid out in Mastering the Mental Game, you're creating more and more mental security. By now, hopefully, you're working on finding your *tribe*, creating your posse, and making your connections. That will help with your emotional security. All of this will help you create the quality of life you deserve. And that's the best reward of all.

Spotlight: Radiant Rahaf
Content Creator

I MET Rahaf during the grimmest early days of the pandemic. She's hard to miss, what with her turquoise hair and her turquoise Mini-Cooper and her ever-present smile. Rahaf is what you'd call radiant. I think it's because she's living her best life. Pay very close attention when you come into contact with someone like this. Some of their sparkle dust just might fall off onto you.

Rahaf has crafted a unique and multi-faceted career for herself that feeds her until she's positively radiating joy and peace and clarity of purpose. She is a content creator. And a sponsored skateboarder. And a part-time college professor (age 36), studying for her PhD in psychology. She came to all this through her first love—skateboarding.

She isn't one of these pros who grew up skating on Venice Beach from the age of five. In fact, she never had a board until she was twenty-six. "I was born in Jordan, and that culture has a lot of really strong gender roles. So my parents put me in ballet and dance and 'things girls do.'" The name, Rahaf, in fact, means "delicate, fine." "And skate-boarding" (like television directing, ahem) "is still mostly male-dominated."

But the day she bought her first skateboard was an epiphany. "I rode it all the way home and I didn't fall once. And it was six miles!" She knew this was what she was meant to do. "That was when I realized I could feel like this. In flow."

Once she experienced flow, she decided she wanted to live that way, have that feeling, in all areas of her life. "I designed a life around flow, so that I can feel like that all the time."

Rahaf "took an inventory of where the energy leaks were in my life" and decided she'd had enough of certain things. She was a server and found that to be her greatest energy drain. So she went to school to get her master's degree in psychology, thinking maybe she could learn more about this flow state and help others achieve it too. But she found she didn't like practicing therapy. "I just couldn't make myself do it. I didn't like having to judge someone so quickly and make assessments about them."

She started *teaching* a few classes, "and that was *closer*, but I was still teaching *therapy*, and that wasn't quite right for me."

She decided to work with a life-coach, and bang! There it was. "I was overflowing with joy." After her skateboarding epiphany, she knew to pay attention to this feeling and decided to become a life-coach herself.

She already was a content creator about skateboarding. Why not use that to build a platform as a life-coach too? And it's worked for her. Really, really well. Her business is scaling fast, and she's coaching and leading workshops for people all over the world.

I'm sure a lot of you reading this would love to be a content creator like Rahaf, who's on her way to 100k followers. But make no mistake: Rahaf *had something to say.* She's not a creator for the sake of looking at herself on the internet. She started posting about skateboarding because she loves it so, so much and wanted to share that joy. She started posting about her life-coaching for the same reason. But she will tell you it has been a journey for her to have an intention that pure. And, like Tammy, the stills photographer in Northern California, noticed, *intention* is really important for your future success.

Rahaf explains it this way: "At first I was thinking about 'How much money can I make doing this?' But you have to shift your intention. Instead, I started asking myself 'How many people can I impact [in a positive way] by doing this?'" Once she shifted her focus, her business grew exponentially.

She echoes what my friend Crystal, the fine artist you read about earlier, meant when she said, "People approach it backwards. They worry about making a living first," putting doing what they love in a secondary position. "You have to just do what you love and worry about the rest later."

A book I read in the beginning of my career that I found very helpful was Marsha Sinetar's *Do What You Love; the Money Will Follow.* I've always believed that.

Rahaf embodies this philosophy. "You never have to worry about the HOW. You [just] have to get really clear with your intention."

If you are on your right path, the HOW will work itself out. It will. You'll learn as you go. We put so much pressure on ourselves to know HOW to do every step along the way to our dream. And, as Rahaf points out, "So many times we get bogged down in thinking there's only one option." There's not. The universe (or God, or the Divine, or however you think of it) can imagine much bigger than you can, by the way. Ask anyone who's enjoying a successful creative career, and though there are some commonalities, you'll learn we've all had a really different path to get to our place of right work.

Chapter Sixteen

You've Got This: Borrowing Confidence from Your Future Self

RAHAF IS SO OBVIOUSLY LIVING her best life now, but she'll tell you frankly, "It took a while to get here. I used to have panic attacks and be on antidepressants." Now she's all organic and shining brightly.

She found the discipline to meditate, and when she was feeling anxious—about money, for example—she'd pay attention to what that worry *felt like* in her body. And she learned how to reprogram her body and mind by some effective self-talk.

Rahaf suffered from scarcity mentality. Perhaps you've heard the term. "Scarcity mentality" is a thing—a thing that will block you from receiving the abundance that is yours for the taking. It refers to the belief that you don't have and *won't* have enough. Enough money, time, energy, love, luck, you name it. It's a mindset of negativity, of limitation, a focus on, and fear of, lack. This way of thinking is a habit that can be broken—and must be broken, or it can become self-fulfilling. Which would be a shame, because it just isn't true!

"I used to put just the bare minimum of gas in my gas tank, worrying about money all the time," Rahaf said. Now she understands that the universe doesn't respond well to a scarcity mindset. "It closes our portal." We need to stay open to whatever unexpected gifts come our way, and to be able to create opportunities ourselves. Rahaf has trained herself to look at her fear and say to it, "Nope, I'm good. My mantra is 'The universe always has my back.'"

Another person might encapsulate this thought as "Let go and let God." Whatever it takes for you to talk yourself down from the ledge, do it. Talk to yourself with the kindness and compassion you would use when speaking to a friend who you know is being too hard on herself.

I know how hard it can be to dig deep and come up with the confidence that will serve you when you need it, whether it's about your ability to make a living at your passion or some other big dream of yours. But you've simply got to talk yourself into it until you are in a more confident head space, or you won't make the moves you need to get you there. You've probably heard the saying "Fake it till you make it." Rahaf likes "Make believe until you believe."

I can relate to this. I recall being in another city, on my first big multi-camera shoot (after becoming proficient at single camera shoots), with one of my bosses along for the ride. He was a great boss, but I was used to running my own set without supervision, and the added pressure of having him there watching my performance was amplifying my nerves. I distinctly recall being in the bathroom, right before heading out on set, in front of a large live audience, a big crew (all male, in those days), and my boss. I was nervous, I'd had too much coffee, and I was rushing too much. And I looked in the mirror and said to myself, "Jeannie, slow down. Wash your hands slower. Give yourself that twenty seconds. You need to walk out there and be perceived as someone who is perfectly calm and confident and in control. I did. And the shoot was a success. And I went on to be a multi-camera director for the next twenty years.

I think of it as "Act as if." Act *as if* you are the best person for this job. Because you know what? All my bosses thought I was, or they wouldn't have put me in that position! And honestly, that's really beside the point. I was new at it, and so of course I wasn't as confident as I would have been today, let's say, when I've been directing for twenty-five years —LOL! We need to give ourselves a break when we are new at something and growing. Of course you're scared! That shows you're stretching your abilities! Good for you! No pain no gain. Growth is always painful! Feel the pain. It won't kill you, I promise. But feel the pain and do it anyway.

I like how Rahaf encapsulates this: "You may have to borrow [confidence] from your future self."

Or sometimes you can borrow it from someone else.

I distinctly remember when I was an associate producer on a show (age twenty-four), looking up to the producers. I was thinking, *I could never do that job. It's just too much: too much responsibility, too many people to supervise, too many elements to budget and schedule, just too many moving parts. I don't know how those producers do it all,* when one of those very producers said to me, "Well, the next thing you should be thinking about is becoming a producer." *She* thought I could do it.

And of course, I did. And really, not too long after that I was able to walk onto the set confidently because I knew I was one of the best producers on the show. In fact, years later, one of my colleagues from those early days was heard telling someone, "Oh, she's a producer's producer."

I'll never forget the first time an Executive Producer said, "You're an excellent director." Or a writer told me that a Show Runner I worked under said, "I love working with Jeannie O'Neill because she's a director who really thinks outside the box."

I tell these anecdotes not to brag, but to let you know that you WILL be in a better place with your endeavors later on, provided you are committed to being excellent. So why not borrow a little courage from that future version of yourself to calm yourself down now, and tell yourself "I can do this." Bridge that gap with the future you.

I can hear you! I can hear you object: "I can SAY those things, but I don't really BELIEVE THEM." This is where meditation or just getting quiet really helps. Sit down, close your eyes, and slow down for a minute, and try to feel how those words/thoughts feel *in your body*. "I can do this." THAT'S the energy you want to tap into.

Look, I don't claim to know exactly how it works—but it does. Swear. This stuff is powerful.

Rahaf puts it this way: "It will sound foreign to you because Present You hasn't grabbed it yet. You know the best version of you wants it; that's all you need to know."

Conclusion

How long are you gonna be dead?

I'm serious.

If you've never thought about that, take a minute and think about it now. Or as poet Mary Oliver puts it, "What is it you plan to do with your one wild and precious life?"

I hope you can hear what beats in your heart. Maybe you were one of the lucky ones who knew all along. It's like that for some of us. (I recall Late Show host Seth Meyers saying that when he discovered improv, his first thought was, *I'm just gonna keep doing this until someone stops me.*) Now you have the tools to mitigate some of the fear that can come with following that exciting energy. It's a little like being in love. Being in love is wonderful, but it can be scary too. A lot of joy comes with it, to be sure, but some pain too, right? Some nervousness? Some stakes?

But don't you think it's worth it? So then, is it suffering? To let your heart lead you to the path you know you want to be on? Or is real suffering *not* being true to yourself? If you're unsure, I recommend the international bestseller by Australian author Bronnie Ware, *The Top Five Regrets of the Dying*. Don't be put off by the title: It's instructional for choosing to live your authentic life NOW so that you won't have regrets later.

The rewards for being on your right path, living a life in sync with your own values and vision, are not to be underestimated. Perhaps that's why so many sages wrote about it. Rumi. Thoreau. Shakespeare. And what *about* Hamlet?! Why did that play's wisdom and popularity endure for hundreds of years? You know the most famous soliloquy: "To be or not to be. That is the question. Whether 'tis nobler to suffer the slings and arrows of outrageous fortune, or to take arms against a sea of troubles, and by opposing them, end them."

Now PRESENT YOU is armed with tools to dispel some of the slings and arrows you will encounter while crafting an unconventional career path for yourself. Believe me, FUTURE YOU will thank you.

The rewards for me have included having interesting work that is intellectually stimulating, creatively satisfying, and usually emotionally satisfying as well. And collaborating with other creatives in diverse settings is a great joy for me. But I think one of the biggest rewards has been TIME.

In this country, it's easier to make money than it is to get TIME. And if the pandemic taught us anything, I'm hoping it taught us that quality of life is *everything*. I think more and more people have woken up to the fact that maybe what they need, *really, really* need, isn't more money, it's more time. Time to do what they love, with whom they love, where they love to be. And maybe now they are making choices more in line with this new value. I sure hope so.

By following the energy, and choosing a career path that is, admittedly, unstable, I have supported myself working *way* less than the traditional forty hours a week, fifty weeks a year. I give myself the gift of time.

Personally, I have always thought that Americans work way too much. No other country in the civilized world (except for Japan, where they actually have a word for "death by overworking."—contemplate *that* for a minute) works as relentlessly as we do. Oh, the many friends who couldn't join me on my travels over the years because their workplaces wouldn't allow them the time off. Is that the lifestyle you want?

RESPECT YOUR PRIORITIES, REAP THE REWARDS

Even when I had a steady job in my twenties on a hit TV show and was allowed the standard two weeks paid vacation (which, in TV, is NOT a standard, but in fact an extreme rarity), I asked for an additional two weeks, unpaid, so I could backpack around New Zealand for a month. Do you think I regret not making the few thousand dollars I could have made those two weeks? Or do you think backpacking around New Zealand was something I'll remember forever and that benefited me for my whole life?

I also was able to fulfill a twenty-year dream of going on safari in Africa. I wanted to go to several African countries, for a month, at least. This is not how Americans typically travel. So when I knew I'd be directing a Discovery Channel

series for a whole six months, I planned a grand tour of
Africa for when the gig ended. And I was able to find a TV
editor friend who was also wrapping a gig to join me. In my
experience, that was pretty rare too—to have a travel buddy
who could take a month off, and the SAME month. That's
hard to find.

As it happened, when I was wrapping the job, the
company offered me another show to direct. It would have
been months of work, on a successful series, with a boss I
liked.

But I wouldn't get to go to Africa.

My cameraman thought I was crazy to turn it down.
"Dude," he said, "you could make a hundred grand this
year!"

"I don't need a hundred grand. I need to go to Africa."
And I did.

(I know. I can hear you thinking: "How nice for *her*. She
was comfortable enough that she felt she didn't need the
money." I get it. Again, this was when I was forty, and had
saved for two decades, not when I was starting out.)

There was a phrase circulating in the culture a lot at the
time: "Don't leave money on the table." Well, I did. And I do.
And I always will—if taking it is not in line with my values
and my heart's desire.

My colleague, Nora, is a television producer in her early
thirties. She had a steady gig on a popular series I was
directing episodes of. And she got invited to a wedding in
Argentina. She hadn't accrued the vacation time needed, but
she decided she was going on the trip, with or without the
boss's permission. She knew she was risking being fired, and
she was okay with that. "Bravo," I told her. "You can always

find another low-budget, nonfiction TV show to work on. But you will never have this wedding in Argentina with all your friends at this age again."

I recall another, more senior producer I worked with who did not attend her sister's wedding, because of work. And I recall it being perceived as a badge of honor among the staff: she was so dedicated to the job, she couldn't *possibly* be away during the season. You decide who you want to be. I want to be Nora.

An important choice for me has been foreign travel. But really, it's quality of life. That's what I'm advocating here. Design a life that delivers the quality of life *you* want.

My friend Courtney has done this successfully. She works on trade shows. For years she has had one client who employs her nine months of the year. The other three months she picks up seasonal work as a tour guide in Alaska. She loves nature and people, and the Alaska gig makes her heart sing.

My colleague, Seth, from Boston, found a job on an American TV show he can produce and direct while living in Bangkok. He finds and pitches his own stories for the show in Southeast Asia because he enjoys the quality of life he has living there.

Now more than ever there are so many opportunities to have a creative career and be a digital nomad! My pal Athena is one. She sold her house, created a following, and posts artistic photos of herself in front of beautiful scenic backdrops the world over, while also giving talks at MIT, Harvard, and the like, about the virtual reality company she's founded.

I could go on and on. The point is, all these artists are

examples of using the tools I've laid out in this book to craft careers that deliver on quality of life for them. And so can you, whatever that looks like for you.

"FAITH. HOPE. AND LOVE. AND THE GREATEST OF THESE IS LOVE."

I'm not much for hoping. I'm more down with Oprah's philosophy, which is "Luck is preparation meeting opportunity." I think that's pretty good. Or Ashton Kutcher's graduation speech that blew up on YouTube. Check that out. What Oprah calls "preparation," he calls "hard work." I don't care what you call it. I know what it is. I do it. Consistently. And it's given me the lifestyle of my dreams.

"Ms. O'Neill, your camel has arrived."

Now, these were words I never thought I'd hear.

I mean, really. I'm a city girl, through and through. Until I was seventeen, I'd never been further afield than the wine country. And here I was in India, heading out to ride my camel into the desert at sunset. It was breathtaking.

I share this story for a reason:

No matter who you are, or where you come from, you can have some amazing experiences beyond your wildest dreams.

My dream was to travel the world while enjoying a long career in TV. And I have. But your dream doesn't have to be anything like mine. Yours could be to be a content creator, or have a singing career, or write your book from your vacation home on Lake Como. Armed with the tools laid out in this book, and perhaps a mindset shift or two, I hope you feel empowered to make your particular dreams come true. I leave you with my favorite quote from Thoreau:

"If one advances confidently, in the direction of his own dreams and endeavors, to live the life that HE has imagined, he will meet with a success unimagined in common hours."

That is my wish for you.

Carpe Diem.

Acknowledgments

I am sincerely grateful for the creatives who agreed to be interviewed for this book. Thank you for your generosity of spirit and sharing your stories with me.

I am deeply grateful to the novelist Andrew Van Wey, my friend and mentor for the publishing process, and whose successes as an independent author are an inspiration to me.